59th Annual Meeting of the Association for Computational Linguistics and the 11th International Joint Conference on Natural Language Processing (ACL-IJCNLP 2021)

Tutorial Abstracts

Online
1 August 2021

ISBN: 978-1-7138-3312-3

Printed from e-media with permission by:

Curran Associates, Inc.
57 Morehouse Lane
Red Hook, NY 12571

Some format issues inherent in the e-media version may also appear in this print version.

Printed with permission by Curran Associates, Inc. (2021)

For permission requests, please contact the Association for Computational Linguistics at the address below.

Association for Computational Linguistics
209 N. Eighth Street
Stroudsburg, Pennsylvania 18360

Phone: 1-570-476-8006
Fax: 1-570-476-0860

acl@aclweb.org

Additional copies of this publication are available from:

Curran Associates, Inc.
57 Morehouse Lane
Red Hook, NY 12571 USA
Phone: 845-758-0400
Fax: 845-758-2633
Email: curran@proceedings.com
Web: www.proceedings.com

ACL-IJCNLP 2021

The 59th Annual Meeting of the Association for Computational Linguistics and The 11th International Joint Conference on Natural Language Processing

Tutorial Abstracts

1 August 2021
Bangkok, Thailand (online)

Preface

Tutorials are an opportunity for ACL-IJCNLP attendees, both newcomers and old hands, to be introduced to various topics by people doing cutting-edge research in those topics. As in previous years, tutorials were selected by a unified review process across four conferences (ACL-IJCNLP, EACL, NAACL, and EMNLP). This year, we received 35 submissions, of which six were selected for presentation at ACL-IJCNLP 2021. We're very pleased to have tutorials from experts from all around the world on a diverse range of applications and techniques in NLP, and hope they will be of great benefit to our community.

We would like to thank Xiangyu Duan for preparing this proceedings volume, and Jing-Shin Chang, Yvette Graham, and Yuki Arase for their hard work coordinating the publications process.

David Chiang, University of Notre Dame
Min Zhang, Soochow University
ACL-IJCNLP 2021 Tutorial Co-Chairs

Tutorial Co-Chairs:

David Chiang, University of Notre Dame, USA
Min Zhang, Soochow University, China

Table of Contents

Conference Program

Sunday, August 1, 2021 [UTC+0]

08/01 13:00–14:00	*Advances in Debating Technologies: Building AI That Can Debate Humans* Roy Bar-Haim, Liat Ein-Dor, Matan Orbach, Elad Venezian and Noam Slonim
07/31 23:00–08/01 03:00	*Event-Centric Natural Language Processing* Muhao Chen, Hongming Zhang, Qiang Ning, Manling Li, Heng Ji, Kathleen McKeown and Dan Roth
08/01 13:00–17:00	*Meta Learning and Its Applications to Natural Language Processing* Hung-yi Lee, Ngoc Thang Vu and Shang-Wen Li
08/01 02:00–03:00 and 13:00–14:00	*Pre-training Methods for Neural Machine Translation* Mingxuan Wang and Lei Li
07/31 23:00–08/01 03:00 and 08/01 13:00–17:00	*Prosody: Models, Methods, and Applications* Nigel Ward and Gina-Anne Levow
08/01 13:00–14:00	*Recognizing Multimodal Entailment* Cesar Ilharco, Afsaneh Shirazi, Arjun Gopalan, Arsha Nagrani, Blaz Bratanic, Chris Bregler, Christina Funk, Felipe Ferreira, Gabriel Barcik, Gabriel Ilharco, Georg Osang, Jannis Bulian, Jared Frank, Lucas Smaira, Qin Cao, Ricardo Marino, Roma Patel, Thomas Leung and Vaiva Imbrasaite

Advances in Debating Technologies: Building AI That Can Debate Humans

Roy Bar-Haim Liat Ein-Dor Matan Orbach Elad Venezian Noam Slonim
IBM Research
{roybar, liate, matano, eladv, noams}@il.ibm.com

1 Tutorial Description

1.1 Background and Goals

Argumentation and debating are fundamental capabilities of human intelligence. They are essential for a wide range of everyday activities that involve reasoning, decision making or persuasion. *Computational Argumentation* is defined as "the application of computational methods for analyzing and synthesizing argumentation and human debate" (Gurevych et al., 2016). Over the last few years, this field has been rapidly evolving, as evident by the growing research community, and the increasing number of publications in top NLP and AI conferences.

The tutorial focuses on *Debating Technologies*, a sub-field of computational argumentation defined as "computational technologies developed directly to enhance, support, and engage with human debating" (Gurevych et al., 2016). A recent milestone in this field is *Project Debater*, which was revealed in 2019 as the first AI system that can debate human experts on complex topics.[1] Project Debater is the third in the series of IBM Research AI's grand challenges, following Deep Blue and Watson. It has been developed for over six years by a large team of researchers and engineers, and its live demonstration in February 2019 received massive media attention. This research effort has resulted in more than 50 scientific papers to date, and many datasets freely available for research purposes.

In this tutorial, we aim to answer the question: "what does it take to build a system that can debate humans"? Our main focus is on the scientific problems such system must tackle. Some of these intriguing problems include argument retrieval for a given debate topic, argument quality assessment and stance classification, identifying relevant principled arguments to be used in conjunction with corpus-mined arguments, organizing the arguments into a compelling narrative, recognizing the arguments made by the human opponent and making a rebuttal. For each of these problems we will present relevant scientific work from various research groups as well as our own. Many of the underlying capabilities of Project Debater have been made freely available for academic research, and the tutorial will include a detailed explanation of how to use and leverage these tools.

A complementary goal of the tutorial is to provide a holistic view of a debating system. Such a view is largely missing in the academic literature, where each paper typically addresses a specific problem in isolation. We present a complete pipeline of a debating system, and discuss the information flow and the interaction between the various components. We will also share our experience and lessons learned from developing such a complex, large scale NLP system. Finally, the tutorial will discuss practical applications and future challenges of debating technologies.

1.2 Contents

In this section we provide more details about the contents of the tutorial. The tutorial outline and estimated schedule are listed in Section 3.

Introduction. The tutorial first provides an introduction to computational argumentation. It then introduces the Project Debater grand challenge and provides a high-level view of the building blocks that comprise a debating system.

The next parts of the tutorial describe each of these building blocks in depth.

Argument mining. The core of a debating system is *argument mining* – finding relevant arguments and argument components (claim/conclusion, evidence/premise) for a given

[1] https://www.research.ibm.com/artificial-intelligence/project-debater/

Proceedings of the Joint Conference of the 59th Annual Meeting of the Association for Computational Linguistics and the 11th International Joint Conference on Natural Language Processing: Tutorial Abstracts, pages 1–5, August 1st, 2021.

debate topic, either in a given article, or in a large corpus.

Argument evaluation and analysis. The next tasks in the pipeline involve analysis of the extracted arguments. *Argument quality assessment* aims to select the more convincing arguments. *Stance classification* aims to distinguish between arguments that support our side in the debate and those supporting the opponent's side.

Modeling human dilemma. A complementary source for argumentation that is widely used by professional human debaters is *principled arguments*, which are relevant for a wide variety of topics. A common example is the *black market* argument, potentially relevant in the context of debates on banning a specific product or a service (e.g., *"we should ban alcohol"*). By this argument, imposing a ban leads to the creation of a black market, which in turn makes products or services obtained therein less safe, leads to exploitation, attracts criminal elements, and so on. We discuss recent work on creating a taxonomy of common principled arguments and automatically matching relevant arguments from this taxonomy to a given debate topic.

Listening comprehension and rebuttal. In addition to presenting one side of the debate, engaging in a competitive debate further requires a debating system to effectively rebut arguments raised by the human opponent. The system must listen to an argumentative speech in real-time, understand the main arguments, and produce persuasive counter-arguments.

The nature of the argumentation domain and the characteristics of competitive debates make the understanding of such spoken content challenging. Expressed ideas often span multiple, non-consecutive sentences and many arguments are alluded to rather than explicitly stated. Further difficulty stems from the requirement to identify and rebut the most important parts of a speech that is several minutes long. This contrasts with today's conversational agents, which aim at understanding a single functional command from short inputs.

Core NLP capabilities. This section describes several core NLP capabilities developed as part of Project Debater, including thematic clustering, highly scalable Wikification and semantic similarity for phrases and Wikipedia concepts.

From arguments to narrative. A debating system must arrange the arguments obtained from various sources (arguments mined from a corpus, principled arguments, and counter arguments for rebuttal) into a coherent and persuasive narrative that would keep the audience's attention for several minutes. This section describes the various steps in the narrative generation pipeline. We also discuss the role of humor in keeping a debate lively.

Moving forward – applications and implications. In this part we discuss possible applications and future directions for debating technologies. As an example, we present *Speech by Crowd*, a platform for crowdsourcing decision support. This platform collects arguments from large audiences on debatable topics and generates meaningful narratives summarizing the arguments for each side of the debate. We also discuss *Key Point Analysis*, a novel method for extracting the main points in a large collection of arguments, and quantifying the prevalence of each point in the data.

Demo session - using debating technologies in your application. Many of the Project Debater components presented in this tutorial have been recently released as cloud APIs, and are freely available for academic use.[2] In the final part of the tutorial, we provide an overview of these APIs, and demonstrate their use for building practical applications.

1.3 Relevance to the Computational Linguistics Community

The tutorial is relevant to a broad audience of NLP researchers and practitioners, working on problems related to argumentation mining, stance classification, discourse analysis, text summarization, NLG, dialogue systems, and more.

2 Tutorial Type

This is a *cutting-edge* tutorial. The main difference between this tutorial and previous tutorials on computational argumentation or argument mining (Slonim et al., 2016; Budzynska and Reed, 2019) is that we focus on the science behind *debating systems* — systems that can engage in a live debate with humans. Accordingly, a large portion of the tutorial's topics, e.g., listening comprehension, rebuttal, narrative generation and modeling

[2]`https://early-access-program.debater.res.ibm.com/academic_use`

human dilemma, was not covered in previous tutorials. Some of the topics, like argument mining, argument quality and stance classification were previously discussed in the tutorial of Slonim et al. (2016), however we will mostly focus on more recent advancements in these areas. The tutorial of Budzynska and Reed (2019) focused on argument structure parsing based on argumentation theory, which can be viewed as complementary to the content of the current tutorial.

3 Outline and Estimated Schedule

Part 1: Introduction (20 min)

- What is Computational Argumentation?
- Project Debater - AI that can debate human experts; outside the AI comfort zone
- Building blocks: decomposing the grand challenge

Part 2: Argument Mining (25 min)

- What is argument mining?
- Identification of argument components
- Document-level vs. sentence level approach
- Corpus-wide argument mining
- Debate topic expansion
- Token-level argument mining

Part 3: Argument Evaluation and Analysis (25 min)

- Argument stance classification
- Argument quality

Part 4: Modeling Human Dilemma (15 min)

- Common principled arguments
- When do principled arguments apply?

Coffee break

Part 5: Listening Comprehension and Rebuttal (25 min)

- Debate vs. classical conversation systems
- Understanding the gist of long, spontaneous speech
- From understanding to rebuttal

Part 6: Core NLP capabilities (10 min)

- Thematic clustering
- Wikification
- Multi-word and concept-level similarity

Part 7: From Arguments to Narrative (10 min)

- Narrative generation pipeline: argument filtering, redundancy removal, clustering, theme extraction, rephrasing and speech generation
- Keeping a live debate lively: the importance of humor

Part 8: Moving Forward – Applications and Implications (20 min)

- Possible applications
- Speech by crowd
- Key point analysis
- Future directions

Part 9: Demo Session - Using Debating Technologies in Your Application (30 min)

- Overview of Project Debater APIs
- Usage examples

4 Prerequisites

The tutorial will be self-contained. We assume basic knowledge of NLP and machine learning, at the level of introductory courses in these areas.

5 Reading List

1. A survey on argument mining: Lawrence and Reed (2019)
2. Project Debater: Slonim et al. (2021)
3. Identification of argument components within an article: Levy et al. (2014), Rinott et al. (2015), Lippi and Torroni (2015)
4. Corpus-wide argument mining: Stab et al. (2018), Ein-Dor et al. (2020)
5. Argument quality: Wachsmuth et al. (2017), Habernal and Gurevych (2016)
6. Stance classification: Bar-Haim et al. (2017)
7. Modeling human dilemma: Bilu et al. (2019)
8. Listening Comprehension: Mirkin et al. (2018)

6 Tutorial Presenters

- Roy Bar-Haim, IBM Research AI
  roybar@il.ibm.com
  https://researcher.watson.ibm.com/researcher/view.php?person=il-ROYBAR
- Liat Ein-Dor, IBM Research AI
  liate@il.ibm.com
  https://researcher.watson.ibm.com/researcher/view.php?person=il-LIATE
- Matan Orbach, IBM Research AI
  matano@il.ibm.com
  https://researcher.watson.ibm.com/researcher/view.php?person=il-MATANO
- Elad Venezian, IBM Research AI
  eladv@il.ibm.com
  https://researcher.watson.ibm.com/researcher/view.php?person=il-ELADV
- Noam Slonim, IBM Research AI
  noams@il.ibm.com
  https://researcher.watson.ibm.com/researcher/view.php?person=il-NOAMS

Roy Bar-Haim is a Research Staff Member at IBM Research AI. Since joining Project Debater in 2013, he has been leading a global research team working on stance classification, sentiment analysis, argument mining and argument summarization. He has published in leading NLP and AI conferences and journals, including ACL, EMNLP, AAAI, COLING, EACL, JAIR and JNLE. He regularly reviews for top NLP and AI conferences, and serves as a member of the TACL elite reviewer team. Roy received his Ph.D in Computer Science from Bar-Ilan University. Before joining IBM, he led NLP research teams in several startup companies. Roy delivered a one-hour talk about Project Debater at the NeurIPS 2018 Expo.

Liat Ein-Dor is a Research Staff Member at IBM Research AI. She received her Ph.D in theoretical physics from Bar-Ilan University in 2001 and has taught several courses there. In 2002 she was a postdoctoral fellow in Laboratoire de Physique Théorique de l'Ecole Normale Supérieure Paris, and from 2003 to 2006 she was a Postdoctoral Fellow and a Research Consultant at the Weizmann Institute of Science. Since 2006, Liat has been working as a research scientist in the hi-tech industry, and joined IBM's Haifa Research Lab in 2010. She has been leading research activities within Project Debater on tasks such as semantic similarity and argumentation mining. She has a diverse background in machine learning, having worked on a variety of domains including computational linguistics, computational biology, fraud detection and theoretical physics. She has publications in all these fields.

Matan Orbach is a Research Staff Member at IBM Research AI. Since joining IBM in 2014, he has worked on a diverse set of NLP tasks, recently focusing on multilingual stance detection and targeted sentiment analysis. Within Project Debater, Matan has led a team working on rebuttal generation through the use of principled arguments. Prior to joining IBM, he received his M.Sc. from the faculty of Electrical Engineering at the Technion, where his research focused on graph-based semi-supervised learning.

Elad Venezian is a Research Staff Member at IBM Research AI. He is currently the chief architect of Project Debater with a focus on making Project Debater technologies available to academia and business. Prior to this role, Elad served in different technical and leadership roles in the Project Debater grand challenge, among them, leading the speech generation team. Elad received his M.Sc. from the faculty of Electrical Engineering at the Tel Aviv University, where his research focused on non-linear systems.

Noam Slonim is a Distinguished Engineer at IBM Research AI. He received his doctorate from the Interdisciplinary Center for Neural Computation at the Hebrew University and held a post-doc position at the Genomics Institute at Princeton University. Noam proposed to develop Project Debater in 2011. He has been serving as the Principal Investigator of the project since then. Noam published around 60 peer reviewed articles, focusing on the last few years on advancing the emerging field of Computational Argumentation. Noam initiated and co-organized the ACL-2016 tutorial on NLP Approaches to Computational Argumentation and the 2015 Dagstuhl workshop on Debating Technologies. In EMNLP 2018 he co-chaired the Argument Mining workshop. Noam delivered a keynote speech on Project Debater at EMNLP 2019.

References

Roy Bar-Haim, Indrajit Bhattacharya, Francesco Dinuzzo, Amrita Saha, and Noam Slonim. 2017. Stance classification of context-dependent claims. In *Proceedings of the 15th Conference of the European Chapter of the Association for Computational Linguistics: Volume 1, Long Papers*, pages 251–261, Valencia, Spain. Association for Computational Linguistics.

Yonatan Bilu, Ariel Gera, Daniel Hershcovich, Benjamin Sznajder, Dan Lahav, Guy Moshkowich, Anael Malet, Assaf Gavron, and Noam Slonim. 2019. Argument invention from first principles. In *Proceedings of the 57th Annual Meeting of the Association for Computational Linguistics*, pages 1013–1026, Florence, Italy. Association for Computational Linguistics.

Katarzyna Budzynska and Chris Reed. 2019. Advances in argument mining. In *Proceedings of the 57th Annual Meeting of the Association for Computational Linguistics: Tutorial Abstracts*, pages 39–42, Florence, Italy. Association for Computational Linguistics.

Liat Ein-Dor, Eyal Shnarch, Lena Dankin, Alon Halfon, Benjamin Sznajder, Ariel Gera, Carlos Alzate, Martin Gleize, Leshem Choshen, Yufang Hou, Yonatan Bilu, Ranit Aharonov, and Noam Slonim. 2020. Corpus wide argument mining - A working solution. In *Proceedings of the Thirty-Fourth AAAI Conference on Artificial Intelligence*, pages 7683–7691. AAAI Press.

Iryna Gurevych, Eduard H. Hovy, Noam Slonim, and Benno Stein. 2016. Debating Technologies (Dagstuhl Seminar 15512). *Dagstuhl Reports*, 5(12):18–46.

Ivan Habernal and Iryna Gurevych. 2016. Which argument is more convincing? analyzing and predicting convincingness of web arguments using bidirectional LSTM. In *Proceedings of the 54th Annual Meeting of the Association for Computational Linguistics (Volume 1: Long Papers)*, pages 1589–1599, Berlin, Germany. Association for Computational Linguistics.

John Lawrence and Chris Reed. 2019. Argument mining: A survey. *Computational Linguistics*, 45(4):765–818.

Ran Levy, Yonatan Bilu, Daniel Hershcovich, Ehud Aharoni, and Noam Slonim. 2014. Context dependent claim detection. In *Proceedings of COLING 2014, the 25th International Conference on Computational Linguistics: Technical Papers*, pages 1489–1500, Dublin, Ireland. Dublin City University and Association for Computational Linguistics.

Marco Lippi and Paolo Torroni. 2015. Context-independent claim detection for argument mining. In *Proceedings of the 24th International Conference on Artificial Intelligence*, IJCAI'15, pages 185–191. AAAI Press.

Shachar Mirkin, Guy Moshkowich, Matan Orbach, Lili Kotlerman, Yoav Kantor, Tamar Lavee, Michal Jacovi, Yonatan Bilu, Ranit Aharonov, and Noam Slonim. 2018. Listening comprehension over argumentative content. In *Proceedings of the 2018 Conference on Empirical Methods in Natural Language Processing*, pages 719–724, Brussels, Belgium. Association for Computational Linguistics.

Ruty Rinott, Lena Dankin, Carlos Alzate Perez, Mitesh M. Khapra, Ehud Aharoni, and Noam Slonim. 2015. Show me your evidence - an automatic method for context dependent evidence detection. In *Proceedings of the 2015 Conference on Empirical Methods in Natural Language Processing*, pages 440–450, Lisbon, Portugal. Association for Computational Linguistics.

Noam Slonim, Yonatan Bilu, Carlos Alzate, Roy Bar-Haim, Ben Bogin, Francesca Bonin, Leshem Choshen, Edo Cohen-Karlik, Lena Dankin, Lilach Edelstein, Liat Ein-Dor, Roni Friedman-Melamed, Assaf Gavron, Ariel Gera, Martin Gleize, Shai Gretz, Dan Gutfreund, Alon Halfon, Daniel Hershcovich, Ron Hoory, Yufang Hou, Shay Hummel, Michal Jacovi, Charles Jochim, Yoav Kantor, Yoav Katz, David Konopnicki, Zvi Kons, Lili Kotlerman, Dalia Krieger, Dan Lahav, Tamar Lavee, Ran Levy, Naftali Liberman, Yosi Mass, Amir Menczel, Shachar Mirkin, Guy Moshkowich, Shila Ofek-Koifman, Matan Orbach, Ella Rabinovich, Ruty Rinott, Slava Shechtman, Dafna Sheinwald, Eyal Shnarch, Ilya Shnayderman, Aya Soffer, Artem Spector, Benjamin Sznajder, Assaf Toledo, Orith Toledo-Ronen, Elad Venezian, and Ranit Aharonov. 2021. An autonomous debating system. *Nature*, 591(7850):379–384.

Noam Slonim, Iryna Gurevych, Chris Reed, and Benno Stein. 2016. NLP approaches to computational argumentation. In *Proceedings of the 54th Annual Meeting of the Association for Computational Linguistics: Tutorial Abstracts*, Berlin, Germany. Association for Computational Linguistics.

Christian Stab, Tristan Miller, Benjamin Schiller, Pranav Rai, and Iryna Gurevych. 2018. Cross-topic argument mining from heterogeneous sources. In *Proceedings of the 2018 Conference on Empirical Methods in Natural Language Processing*, pages 3664–3674, Brussels, Belgium. Association for Computational Linguistics.

Henning Wachsmuth, Nona Naderi, Yufang Hou, Yonatan Bilu, Vinodkumar Prabhakaran, Tim Alberdingk Thijm, Graeme Hirst, and Benno Stein. 2017. Computational argumentation quality assessment in natural language. In *Proceedings of the 15th Conference of the European Chapter of the Association for Computational Linguistics: Volume 1, Long Papers*, pages 176–187, Valencia, Spain. Association for Computational Linguistics.

Event-Centric Natural Language Processing

Muhao Chen[1], Hongming Zhang[2,3], Qiang Ning[4],
Manling Li[5], Heng Ji[4,5], Kathleen McKeown[6], Dan Roth[2]
[1]Department of Computer Science, USC
[2]Department of Computer and Information Science, UPenn
[3]Department of Computer Science and Engineering, HKUST
[4]Amazon Alexa AI
[5]Department of Computer Science, UIUC
[6]Department of Computer Science, Columbia University

Abstract

This tutorial targets researchers and practitioners who are interested in AI technologies that help machines understand natural language text, particularly real-world events described in the text. These include methods to extract the internal structures of an event regarding its protagonist(s), participant(s) and properties, as well as external structures concerning memberships, temporal and causal relations of multiple events. This tutorial will provide audience with a systematic introduction of (i) knowledge representations and acquisition of events, (ii) various methods for automated extraction, conceptualization, coreference resolution and prediction of events and their relations, (iii) induction of event processes and properties, and (iv) a wide range of NLP and commonsense understanding tasks that benefit from aforementioned techniques. We will conclude the tutorial by outlining emerging research problems in this area.

1 Introduction

Human languages always involve the description of real-world events. Therefore, understanding events plays a critical role in NLP. For example, narrative prediction benefits from learning the causal relations of events to predict what happens next in a story (Chaturvedi et al., 2017a); machine comprehension of documents may involve understanding of events that affect the stock market (Ding et al., 2015), describe natural phenomena (Berant et al., 2014) or identify disease phenotypes (Zhang et al., 2020d). In fact, event understanding also widely finds its important use cases in tasks such as open-domain question answering (Yang et al., 2003), intent prediction (Rashkin et al., 2018), timeline construction (Do et al., 2012), text summarization (Daumé III and Marcu, 2006) and misinformation detection (Fung et al., 2021). Since events are not just simple, standalone predicates, frontier research on event understanding generally faces two key challenges. One challenge is to precisely induce the relations of events, which describe memberships, co-reference, temporal orders and causality of events. The other is to comprehend the inherent structure and properties of an event, concerning its participants, granularity, location and time.

In this tutorial, we will comprehensively review existing paradigms for event-centric knowledge representation in literature, and focus on their contributions to NLP tasks. Beyond introducing partial-label and unsupervised learning approaches for event extraction, we will discuss recent constrained learning and structured inference approaches for multi-faceted event-event relation extraction from text. We will also review recent data-driven methods for event prediction tasks, including event process induction and conceptualization, and how an event-centric language model benefits narrative prediction. In addition, we will illustrate how distantly supervised approaches help resolve temporal and causal commonsense understanding of events, and how they can be applied to construct a large-scale eventuality knowledge base. Participants will learn about recent trends and emerging challenges in this topic, representative tools and learning resources to obtain ready-to-use models, and how related models and techniques benefit end-use NLP applications.

2 Outline of Tutorial Content

This **half-day** tutorial presents a systematic overview of recent advances in event-centric NLP technologies. We will begin with motivating this topic with several real-world applications, and introduce the main research problems. Then, we will introduce methods for automated extraction of events as well as their participants, properties and relations from natural language text. Based on the

Proceedings of the Joint Conference of the 59th Annual Meeting of the Association for Computational Linguistics and the 11th International Joint Conference on Natural Language Processing: Tutorial Abstracts, pages 6–14, August 1st, 2021.

extracted eventuality knowledge, we will explain how various prediction tasks, including the completion of an event complex, conceptualization and consolidation of event processes, can be resolved. We will also discuss commonsense understanding of events, with a focus on the temporal and cognitive aspects. Moreover, we will exemplify the use of aforementioned technologies in NLP applications of various domains, and will outline emerging research challenges that may catalyze further investigation on this topic. The detailed contents are outlined below.

2.1 Motivation [20min]

We will define the main research problem and motivate the topic by presenting several real-world applications based on event-centric NLP. This seeks to provide 20 minutes of presented content to motivate the main topic of this tutorial.

2.2 Background of Events and Their Representations [30min]

We will start the tutorial by introducing the essential background knowledge about events and their relations, including the definitions, categorizations, and applications (P. D. Mourelatos, 1978; Bach, 1986). In the last part of the introduction, we will talk about widely used event representation methods, including event schemas (Baker et al., 1998; Li et al., 2020b, 2021a), event knowledge graphs (Zhang et al., 2020c), event processes (Chambers and Jurafsky, 2008), event language models (Peng et al., 2017), and more recent work on event meaning representation via question-answer pairs (He et al., 2015; Michael et al., 2018), event network embeddings (Zeng et al., 2021) and event time expression embeddings (Goyal and Durrett, 2019). This part is estimated to take 30 minutes.

2.3 Event-centric Information Extraction [40min]

We will introduce unsupervised and zero-shot techniques for parsing the internal structures of verb and nominal events from natural language text, which also involves methods for automatic salient event detection (Liu et al., 2018), joint entity, relation and event extraction (Lin et al., 2020), and graph neural networks based encoding and decoding for information extraction (Zhang and Ji, 2021). Then we will discuss the recent research trend to extend information extraction from sentence-level to document-level (Du and Cardie, 2020; Li et al., 2021b). Besides, we will also discuss methods that identify temporal and causal relations of primitive events (Ning et al., 2018), and membership relations of multi-granular events (Aldawsari and Finlayson, 2019). Specifically, for data-driven extraction methods, we will present how constrained learning (Li et al., 2019) and structured prediction are incorporated to improve the tasks by enforcing logic consistency among different categories of event-event relations (Wang et al., 2020). We will also cover various cross-domain (Huang et al., 2018), cross-lingual (Subburathinam et al., 2019) and cross-media (Li et al., 2020a) structure transfer approaches for event extraction. This part is estimated to be 40 minutes.

2.4 Understanding Event Processes [35min]

We will then present recent works on machine comprehension and prediction on event processes/sequences. Specifically, people are trying to understand the progress of events from different angles. For example, many efforts have been devoted into modeling event narratives (Peng et al., 2017; Chaturvedi et al., 2017b; Lee and Goldwasser, 2019) such that they can successfully predict missing events in an event process. Besides, another important event understanding angle is conceptualization (Zhang et al., 2020a), which aims at understanding the super-sub relations between a coarse-grained event and a fine-grained event process (Glavaš et al., 2014). In this context, the machine could also be expected to generate the event process given a goal (Zhang et al., 2020a), infer the goal given the process (Chen et al., 2020), and capture the recurrence of events in a process (Zhu et al., 2021). Last but not least, event coreference, which links references to the same event together, also plays a critical role in understanding events (Cybulska and Vossen, 2014). This part should last for 35 minutes.

2.5 Event-centric Commonsense Knowledge Acquisition [35min]

Commonsense reasoning is a challenging yet important research problem in the AI community and one key challenge we are facing is the lack of satisfactory commonsense knowledge resources about events. Previous resources (Liu and Singh, 2004) typically require laborious and expensive human annotations, which are not feasible on a large scale. In this tutorial, we introduce recent progress on modeling commonsense knowledge with high-order selectional preference over event knowledge and demonstrates that how to convert relatively cheap event knowledge, which can be easily acquired from raw documents with linguistic patterns, to precious commonsense knowledge defined in ConceptNet (Zhang et al., 2020b). Beyond that, we will also introduce how to automatically acquire other event-centric commonsense knowledge including but not limited to temporal properties (Zhou et al., 2020), intentions (Chen et al., 2020), effects (Sap et al., 2019) and graph schemas (Li et al., 2020c) of events. This part is estimated to be 35 minutes.

2.6 Event Summarization [30min]

In addition to specific, individual events, we are also interested in large-scale events that unfold over time. Over the past year, we saw many examples of such events, including COVID-19, the vaccine roll-out, the Black Lives Matter movement and the US presidential election. In this tutorial, we will present methods for tracking such events over time and generating summaries that provide updates as an event unfolds. The task of identifying and tracking events was first introduced in the Topic Detection and Tracking challenge (Allan et al., 1998). Recent work has explored new methods for tracking and visualizing such events over time (e.g., (Laban and Hearst, 2017; Miranda et al., 2018; Staykovski et al., 2019; Saravanakumar et al., 2021)), in some cases generating summaries that contain information on what is new (e.g., (Kedzie et al., 2015, 2018)) and in other cases, exploring timeline summarization, ordering events and generating summaries that are placed along a timeline (e.g., (Wang et al., 2015; Binh Tran et al., 2013; Chen et al., 2019; Nguyen et al., 2014)) We will also consider how these are related to summarization of an event that takes place within a single day, a problem that falls within the category of multi-document summarization (e.g., (Liu and Lapata, 2019; Fabbri et al., 2019)), as typically there may be many articles covering the same event. By using multiple articles as input, a summarizer can present different perspectives on the same event as well as identify salient information that is highlighted many in different ways across the set of input articles. This part is scheduled for 30 minutes

2.7 Emerging Research Problems [20min]

Event-centric NLP impacts on a wide spectrum of knowledge-driven AI tasks, and is particularly knotted with commonsense understanding. We will conclude the tutorial using 20 minutes by presenting some challenges and potential research topics in applying eventuality knowledge in downstream tasks (e.g., reading comprehension, dialogue generation, and event timeline generation), and grounding eventuality knowledge to visual modalities, and challenges for cross-document event consolidation with human-defined schemas.

3 Specification of the Tutorial

The proposed tutorial is considered a **cutting-edge** tutorial that introduces the recent advances in an emerging area of NLP. The presented topic has not been covered by previous ACL/EMNLP/NAACL/EACL/COLING tutorials in the past 4 years. This tutorial has not been presented elsewhere, while a more AI-flavored version with a subset of the contents has been planned in parallel at AAAI 2021, to be presented by a subset of the instructors. We estimate that at least 60% of the works covered in this tutorial are from researchers other than the instructors.

Audience and Prerequisites While no specific background knowledge is assumed of the audience, it would be best for the attendees to know about basic deep learning technologies, pre-trained word embeddings (e.g. Word2Vec) and language models (e.g. BERT). The following is a reading list that could help provide background knowledge to the audience before attending this tutorial:

- Emmon Bach. The algebra of events. Linguistics and philosophy. 9(1):5-16, 1986.
- Nathanael Chambers. Event Schema Induction with a Probabilistic Entity-Driven Model. Proceedings of the 2013 Conference on Empirical Methods in Natural Language Processing (EMNLP), 2013
- Tao Li, Vivek Gupta, Maitrey Mehta, and Vivek Srikumar. A Logic-Driven Framework for Consistency of Neural Models. Proceedings of the 2019 Conference on Empirical Methods in Natural Language Processing and the 9th International Joint Conference on Natural Language Processing (EMNLP-IJCNLP), 2019.

- Ying Lin, Heng Ji, Fei Huang and Lingfei Wu. A Joint Neural Model for Information Extraction with Global Features. Proceedings of the 58th Annual Meeting of the Association for Computational Linguistics (ACL), 2020.

- Haoyu Wang, Muhao Chen, Hongming Zhang, and Dan Roth. Joint Constrained Learning for Event-Event Relation Extraction. Proceedings of the 2020 Empirical Methods in Natural Language Processing (EMNLP), 2020.

- Nathanael Chambers and Dan Jurafsky. Unsupervised learning of narrative event chains. In Proceedings of the 46th Annual Meeting of the Association for Computational Linguistics (ACL), 2008.

- Hongming Zhang, Muhao Chen, Haoyu Wang, Yangqiu Song, and Dan Roth. Open-domain Process Structure Induction. Proceedings of the 2020 Empirical Methods in Natural Language Processing (EMNLP), 2020.;

- Maarten Sap, Ronan Le Bras, Emily Allaway, Chandra Bhagavatula, Nicholas Lourie, Hannah Rashkin, Brendan Roof, Noah A. Smith, and Yejin Choi. Atomic: An atlas of machine commonsense for if-then reasoning. In Proceedings of the AAAI Conference on Artificial Intelligence (AAAI). 2019.

- Ben Zhou, Qiang Ning, Daniel Khashabi, and Dan Roth. Temporal Common Sense Acquisition with Minimal Supervision. Proceedings of the 58th Annual Meeting of the Association for Computational Linguistics (ACL), 2020.

Open Access All the teaching materials are openly available at `https://cogcomp.seas.upenn.edu/page/tutorial.202108/`.

4 Tutorial Instructors

Muhao Chen is an Assistant Research Professor at the Department of Computer Science, USC. Prior to USC, he was a postdoctoral fellow at UPenn. He received his Ph.D. from the Department of Computer Science at UCLA in 2019, and B.S. in Computer Science from Fudan University in 2014. His research focuses on data-driven machine learning approaches for processing structured data, and knowledge acquisition from unstructured data. Particularly, he is interested in developing knowledge-aware learning systems with generalizability and requiring minimal supervision, and with concrete applications to natural language understanding, knowledge base construction, computational biology and medicine. Muhao has published over 40 papers in leading AI, NLP and Comp Bio venues. His work has received a best student paper award at ACM BCB, and a best paper award nomination at CoNLL. Additional information is available at `http://muhaochen.github.io`.

Hongming Zhang is currently a third-year Ph.D. student at HKUST and a visiting scholar at UPenn. Hongming has received Hong Kong Ph.D. Fellowship and Microsoft Research Asia Fellowship to support his research on commonsense reasoning and open domain event understanding. He has published more then ten papers on related topics in top-tier conferences. Additional information is available at `http://www.cse.ust.hk/~hzhangal/`.

Qiang Ning is currently an applied scientist at Alexa AI. Qiang was a research scientist on the AllenNLP team at the Allen Institute for AI from 2019-2020. Qiang received his Ph.D. in Dec. 2019 from the Department of Electrical and Computer Engineering at the University of Illinois at Urbana-Champaign (UIUC). He obtained his master's degree in biomedical imaging from the same department in May 2016. Before coming to the United States, Qiang obtained two bachelor's degrees from Tsinghua University in 2013, in Electronic Engineering and in Economics, respectively. He was an "Excellent Teacher Ranked by Their Students" across the university in 2017 (UIUC), a recipient of the YEE Fellowship in 2015 (College of Engineering at UIUC), a finalist for the best paper in IEEE ISBI'15, and also won the National Scholarship at Tsinghua University in 2012. Additional information is available at `https://qiangning.info/`.

Manling Li is a third-year Ph.D. student at the Computer Science Department of the University of Illinois at Urbana-Champaign (UIUC). Manling has won the Best Demo Paper Award at ACL'20, the Best Demo Paper Award at NAACL'21, C.L. Dave and Jane W.S. Liu Award, and has been selected as Mavis Future Faculty Fellow. She has more than 20 publications on knowledge extraction and reasoning from multimedia data. Additional information is available at `https://limanling.github.io`.

Heng Ji is a Professor at Computer Science Department, and an affiliated faculty member at Electrical and Computer Engineering Department of University of Illinois at Urbana-Champaign. She is also an Amazon Scholar. She received her B.A. and M. A. in Computational Linguistics from Tsinghua University, and her M.S. and Ph.D. in Computer Science from New York University. Her research interests focus on Natural Language Processing, especially on Multimedia Multilingual Information Extraction, Knowledge Base Population and Knowledge-driven Generation. She was selected as "Young Scientist" and a member of the Global Future Council on the Future of Computing by the World Economic Forum in 2016 and 2017. The awards she received include "AI's 10 to Watch" Award by IEEE Intelligent Systems in 2013, NSF CAREER award in 2009, Google Research Award in 2009 and 2014, IBM Watson Faculty Award in 2012 and 2014 and Bosch Research Award in 2014-2018. She was invited by the Secretary of the U.S. Air Force and AFRL to join Air Force Data Analytics Expert Panel to inform the Air Force Strategy 2030. She is the lead of many multi-institution projects and tasks, including the U.S. ARL projects on information fusion and knowledge networks construction, DARPA DEFT Tinker Bell team and DARPA KAIROS RESIN team. She has coordinated the NIST TAC Knowledge Base Population task since 2010. She has served as the Program Committee Co-Chair of many conferences including NAACL-HLT2018. She is elected as the North American Chapter of the Association for Computational Linguistics (NAACL) secretary 2020-2021. Her research has been widely supported by the U.S. government agencies (DARPA, ARL, IARPA, NSF, AFRL, DHS) and industry (Amazon, Google, Bosch, IBM, Disney). Additional information is available at `https://blender.cs.illinois.edu/hengji.html`.

Kathleen R. McKeown is the Henry and Gertrude Rothschild Professor of Computer Science at Columbia University and the Founding Director of the Data Science Institute, serving as Director from 2012 to 2017. She is also an Amazon Scholar. In earlier years, she served as Department Chair (1998-2003) and as Vice Dean for Research for the School of Engineering and Applied Science (2010-2012). A leading scholar and researcher in the field of natural language processing, McKeown focuses her research on the use of data for societal problems; her interests include text summarization, question answering, natural language generation, social media analysis and multilingual applications. She has received numerous honors and awards, including American Academy of Arts and Science elected member, American Association of Artificial Intelligence Fellow, a Founding Fellow of the Association for Computational Linguistics and an Association for Computing Machinery Fellow. Early on she received the National Science Foundation Presidential Young Investigator Award, and a National Science Foundation Faculty Award for Women. In 2010, she won both the Columbia Great Teacher Award—an honor bestowed by the students—and the Anita Borg Woman of Vision Award for Innovation. Additional information is available at `http://www.cs.columbia.edu/~kathy/`.

Dan Roth is the Eduardo D. Glandt Distinguished Professor at the Department of Computer and Information Science, University of Pennsylvania, and a Fellow of the AAAS, ACM, AAAI, and the ACL. In 2017 Roth was awarded the John McCarthy Award, the highest award the AI community gives to mid-career AI researchers. Roth was recognized "for major conceptual and theoretical advances in the modeling of natural language understanding, machine learning, and reasoning." Roth has published broadly in machine learning, natural language processing, knowledge representation and reasoning, and learning theory, and has developed advanced machine learning based tools for natural language applications that are being used widely. Roth has given tutorials on these and other topics in all ACL and AAAI major conferences. Until February 2017 Roth was the Editor-in-Chief of the Journal of Artificial Intelligence Research (JAIR). He was the program chair of AAAI'11, ACL'03 and CoNLL'02, and serves regularly as an area chair and senior program committee member in the major conferences in his research areas. Prof. Roth received his B.A Summa cum laude in Mathematics from the Technion, Israel, and his Ph.D. in Computer Science from Harvard University in 1995. Additional information is available at `http://www.cis.upenn.edu/~danroth/`.

The presenters of this tutorial have given the following tutorials at leading international conferences and venues in the past:

- Muhao Chen:
  - AAAI'21: Event-Centric Natural Language Understanding.
  - AAAI'20: Recent Advances of Transferable

Representation Learning.

- Heng Ji:
  - AAAI'21: Event-Centric Natural Language Understanding.
  - Multi-lingual Entity Discovery and Linking. Tutorial at the 17th China National Conference on Computational Linguistics (CCL2018) and The 6th International Symposium on Natural Language Processing based on Naturally Annotated Big Data (NLP-NABD2018).
  - ACL'18: Multi-lingual Entity Discovery and Linking.
  - Information Extraction and Knowledge Base Population, Invited course for the 10th Russian Summer School in Information Retrieval, 2016.
  - SIGMOD'16: Automatic Entity Recognition and Typing in Massive Text Data.
  - ACL'15: Successful Data Mining Methods for NLP.
  - ACL'14: Wikification and Beyond: The Challenges of Entity and Concept Grounding.
  - Wikification and Beyond: The Challenges of Entity and Concept Grounding, Advanced Disciplines Lecture at NLPCC'14.
  - COLING'12: Temporal Information Extraction and Shallow Temporal Reasoning.
- Kathleen R. McKeown:
  - COLING'86: Natural Language Generation and User Modelling.
  - ACL'86: Natural Language Generation.
- Dan Roth:
  - Data Science Summer Institute (DSSI) 2007, 2008, 2010, 2011, 2012. A tutorial on Machine Learning in Natural Language Processing.
  - AAAI'21: Event-Centric Natural Language Understanding.
  - ACL'20: Commonsense Reasoning for Natural Language Processing.
  - AAAI'20: Recent Advances of Transferable Representation Learning.
  - ACL'18: The Conference of the Association on Computational Linguistics. A tutorial on Multi-lingual Entity Discovery and Linking.
  - EACL'17: The European Conference of the Association of Computational Linguistics; A tutorial on Integer Linear Programming Formulations in Natural Language Processing.
  - AAAI'16: The Conference of the Association for the Advancement of Artificial Intelligence; A tutorial on Structured Prediction.
  - ACL'14: The International Conference of the Association on Computational Linguistics. A tutorial on Wikification and Entity Linking.
  - AAAI'13: The AAAI Conference on Artificial Intelligence. Information Trustworthiness.
  - COLING'12: The International Conference on Computational Linguistics. A Tutorial on Temporal Information Extraction and Shallow Temporal Reasoning.
  - NAACL'12: The North American Conference of the Association on Computational Linguistics. A Tutorial on Constrained Conditional Models: Structured Predictions in NLP.
  - NAACL'10: The North American Conference of the Association on Computational Linguistics. A Tutorial on Integer Linear Programming Methods in NLP.
  - EACL'09: The European Conference of the Association on Computational Linguistics. A Tutorial on Constrained Conditional Models.
  - ACL'07: The International Conference of the Association on Computational Linguistics. A Tutorial on Textual Entailment.

Acknowledgement

This material is based upon work supported in part by U.S. DARPA KAIROS Program Nos. FA8750-19-2-1004, U.S. DARPA AIDA Program No. FA8750-18-2-0014, Air Force Nos. FA8650-17-C-7715 and FA8750-20-2-10002. The views and conclusions contained herein are those of the authors and should not be interpreted as necessarily representing the official policies, either expressed or implied, of DARPA, or the U.S. Government. The U.S. Government is authorized to reproduce and distribute reprints for governmental purposes notwithstanding any copyright annotation therein.

References

Mohammed Aldawsari and Mark Finlayson. 2019. Detecting subevents using discourse and narrative features. In *Proceedings of the 57th Annual Meeting of the Association for Computational Linguistics*, pages 4780–4790, Florence, Italy. Association for Computational Linguistics.

James Allan, Jaime G Carbonell, George Doddington, Jonathan Yamron, and Yiming Yang. 1998. Topic detection and tracking pilot study final report.

Emmon Bach. 1986. The algebra of events. *Linguistics and philosophy*, 9(1):5–16.

Collin F. Baker, Charles J. Fillmore, and John B. Lowe. 1998. The berkeley framenet project. In *COLING-ACL*, pages 86–90.

Jonathan Berant, Vivek Srikumar, Pei-Chun Chen, Abby Vander Linden, Brittany Harding, Brad Huang, Peter Clark, and Christopher D. Manning. 2014. Modeling biological processes for reading comprehension. In *Proceedings of the 2014 Conference on Empirical Methods in Natural Language Processing (EMNLP)*, pages 1499–1510, Doha, Qatar. Association for Computational Linguistics.

Giang Binh Tran, Mohammad Alrifai, and Dat Quoc Nguyen. 2013. Predicting relevant news events for timeline summaries. In *Proceedings of the 22nd International Conference on World Wide Web*, pages 91–92.

Nathanael Chambers and Dan Jurafsky. 2008. Unsupervised learning of narrative event chains. In *Proceedings of ACL-08: HLT*, pages 789–797, Columbus, Ohio. Association for Computational Linguistics.

Snigdha Chaturvedi, Haoruo Peng, and Dan Roth. 2017a. Story comprehension for predicting what happens next. In *Proceedings of the 2017 Conference on Empirical Methods in Natural Language Processing*, pages 1603–1614, Copenhagen, Denmark. Association for Computational Linguistics.

Snigdha Chaturvedi, Haoruo Peng, and Dan Roth. 2017b. Story Comprehension for Predicting What Happens Next. In *In proceedings of the Conference on Empirical Methods in Natural Language Processing*.

Muhao Chen, Hongming Zhang, Haoyu Wang, and Dan Roth. 2020. "what are you trying to do?" semantic typing of event processes. In *Proceedings of the 24th Conference on Computational Natural Language Learning (CoNLL 2020)*. Association for Computational Linguistics.

Xiuying Chen, Zhangming Chan, Shen Gao, Meng-Hsuan Yu, Dongyan Zhao, and Rui Yan. 2019. Learning towards abstractive timeline summarization. In *Proceedings of the Twenty-Eighth International Joint Conference on Artificial Intelligence, IJCAI 2019, Macao, China, August 10-16, 2019*, pages 4939–4945. ijcai.org.

Agata Cybulska and Piek Vossen. 2014. Guidelines for ecb+ annotation of events and their coreference. In *Technical Report*. Technical Report NWR-2014-1, VU University Amsterdam.

Hal Daumé III and Daniel Marcu. 2006. Bayesian query-focused summarization. In *Proceedings of the 21st International Conference on Computational Linguistics and 44th Annual Meeting of the Association for Computational Linguistics*, pages 305–312, Sydney, Australia. Association for Computational Linguistics.

Xiao Ding, Yue Zhang, Ting Liu, and Junwen Duan. 2015. Deep learning for event-driven stock prediction. In *Twenty-fourth international joint conference on artificial intelligence*.

Quang Do, Wei Lu, and Dan Roth. 2012. Joint inference for event timeline construction. In *Proceedings of the 2012 Joint Conference on Empirical Methods in Natural Language Processing and Computational Natural Language Learning*, pages 677–687, Jeju Island, Korea. Association for Computational Linguistics.

Xinya Du and Claire Cardie. 2020. Event extraction by answering (almost) natural questions. In *Proc. The 2020 Conference on Empirical Methods in Natural Language Processing (EMNLP2020)*.

Alexander Fabbri, Irene Li, Tianwei She, Suyi Li, and Dragomir Radev. 2019. Multi-news: A large-scale multi-document summarization dataset and abstractive hierarchical model. In *Proceedings of the 57th Annual Meeting of the Association for Computational Linguistics*, pages 1074–1084, Florence, Italy. Association for Computational Linguistics.

Yi Fung, Christopher Thomas, Revanth Gangi Reddy, Sandeep Polisetty, Heng Ji, Shih-Fu Chang, Kathleen McKeown, Mohit Bansal, and Avi Sil. 2021. Infosurgeon: Cross-media fine-grained information consistency checking for fake news detection. In *Proc. The Joint Conference of the 59th Annual Meeting of the Association for Computational Linguistics and the 11th International Joint Conference on Natural Language Processing (ACL-IJCNLP 2021)*.

Goran Glavaš, Jan Šnajder, Marie-Francine Moens, and Parisa Kordjamshidi. 2014. HiEve: A corpus for extracting event hierarchies from news stories. In *Proceedings of the Ninth International Conference on Language Resources and Evaluation (LREC-2014)*, pages 3678–3683, Reykjavik, Iceland. European Languages Resources Association (ELRA).

Tanya Goyal and Greg Durrett. 2019. Embedding time expressions for deep temporal ordering models. In *Proceedings of the 57th Annual Meeting of the Association for Computational Linguistics 2019 (ACL2019)*.

Luheng He, Mike Lewis, and Luke Zettlemoyer. 2015. Question-answer driven semantic role labeling: Using natural language to annotate natural language. In *Proceedings of the 2015 Conference on Empirical Methods in Natural Language Processing*, pages 643–653.

Lifu Huang, Heng Ji, Kyunghyun Cho, Ido Dagan, Sebastian Riedel, and Clare Voss. 2018. Zero-shot transfer learning for event extraction. In *Proc. The 56th Annual Meeting of the Association for Computational Linguistics (ACL2018)*.

Chris Kedzie, Kathleen McKeown, and Hal Daumé III. 2018. Content selection in deep learning models of summarization. In *Proceedings of the 2018 Conference on Empirical Methods in Natural Language Processing*, pages 1818–1828, Brussels, Belgium. Association for Computational Linguistics.

Chris Kedzie, Kathleen McKeown, and Fernando Diaz. 2015. Predicting salient updates for disaster summarization. In *Proceedings of the 53rd Annual Meeting of the Association for Computational Linguistics and the 7th International Joint Conference on Natural Language Processing (Volume 1: Long Papers)*, pages 1608–1617, Beijing, China. Association for Computational Linguistics.

Philippe Laban and Marti Hearst. 2017. newsLens: building and visualizing long-ranging news stories. In *Proceedings of the Events and Stories in the News Workshop*, pages 1–9, Vancouver, Canada. Association for Computational Linguistics.

I-Ta Lee and Dan Goldwasser. 2019. Multi-relational script learning for discourse relations. In *Proceedings of the 57th Annual Meeting of the Association for Computational Linguistics*, pages 4214–4226, Florence, Italy. Association for Computational Linguistics.

Manling Li, Sha Li, Zhenhailong Wang, Lifu Huang, Kyunghyun Cho, Heng Ji, and Jiawei Han. 2021a. Future is not one-dimensional: Complex event schema induction via graph modeling. In *arxiv2104.06344*.

Manling Li, Alireza Zareian, Qi Zeng, Spencer Whitehead, Di Lu, Heng Ji, and Shih-Fu Chang. 2020a. Cross-media structured common space for multimedia event extraction. In *Proc. The 58th Annual Meeting of the Association for Computational Linguistics (ACL2020)*.

Manling Li, Qi Zeng, Ying Lin, Kyunghyun Cho, Heng Ji, Jonathan May, Nathanael Chambers, and Clare Voss. 2020b. Connecting the dots: Event graph schema induction with path language modeling. In *Proc. The 2020 Conference on Empirical Methods in Natural Language Processing (EMNLP2020)*.

Manling Li, Qi Zeng, Ying Lin, Kyunghyun Cho, Heng Ji, Jonathan May, Nathanael Chambers, and Clare Voss. 2020c. Connecting the dots: Event graph schema induction with path language modeling. In *Proc. The 2020 Conference on Empirical Methods in Natural Language Processing (EMNLP2020)*.

Sha Li, Heng Ji, and Jiawei Han. 2021b. Document-level event argument extraction by conditional generation. In *Proc. The 2021 Conference of the North American Chapter of the Association for Computational Linguistics - Human Language Technologies (NAACL-HLT2021)*.

Tao Li, Vivek Gupta, Maitrey Mehta, and Vivek Srikumar. 2019. A logic-driven framework for consistency of neural models. In *Proceedings of the 2019 Conference on Empirical Methods in Natural Language Processing and the 9th International Joint Conference on Natural Language Processing (EMNLP-IJCNLP)*, pages 3924–3935, Hong Kong, China. Association for Computational Linguistics.

Ying Lin, Heng Ji, Fei Huang, and Lingfei Wu. 2020. A joint neural model for information extraction with global features. In *Proc. The 58th Annual Meeting of the Association for Computational Linguistics (ACL2020)*.

Hugo Liu and Push Singh. 2004. Conceptnet: a practical commonsense reasoning tool-kit. *BT technology journal*, 22(4):211–226.

Jun Liu, Fei Cheng, Yiran Wang, Hiroyuki Shindo, and Yuji Matsumoto. 2018. Automatic error correction on Japanese functional expressions using character-based neural machine translation. In *Proceedings of the 32nd Pacific Asia Conference on Language, Information and Computation*, Hong Kong. Association for Computational Linguistics.

Yang Liu and Mirella Lapata. 2019. Hierarchical transformers for multi-document summarization. In *Proceedings of the 57th Annual Meeting of the Association for Computational Linguistics*, pages 5070–5081, Florence, Italy. Association for Computational Linguistics.

Julian Michael, Gabriel Stanovsky, Luheng He, Ido Dagan, and Luke Zettlemoyer. 2018. Crowdsourcing question-answer meaning representations. In *Proceedings of the 2018 Conference of the North American Chapter of the Association for Computational Linguistics: Human Language Technologies*, pages 560–568.

Sebastião Miranda, Artūrs Znotiņš, Shay B. Cohen, and Guntis Barzdins. 2018. Multilingual clustering of streaming news. In *Proceedings of the 2018 Conference on Empirical Methods in Natural Language Processing*, pages 4535–4544, Brussels, Belgium. Association for Computational Linguistics.

Kiem-Hieu Nguyen, Xavier Tannier, and Veronique Moriceau. 2014. Ranking multidocument event descriptions for building thematic timelines. In *Proceedings of COLING 2014, the 25th International Conference on Computational Linguistics: Technical Papers*, pages 1208–1217, Dublin, Ireland. Dublin City University and Association for Computational Linguistics.

Qiang Ning, Hao Wu, and Dan Roth. 2018. A multi-axis annotation scheme for event temporal relations. In *Proceedings of the 56th Annual Meeting of the Association for Computational Linguistics (Volume 1: Long Papers)*, pages 1318–1328, Melbourne, Australia. Association for Computational Linguistics.

Alexander P. D. Mourelatos. 1978. Events, processes, and states. *Linguistics and Philosophy*, 2:415–434.

Haoruo Peng, Snigdha Chaturvedi, and Dan Roth. 2017. A joint model for semantic sequences: Frames, entities, sentiments. In *Proceedings of the 21st Conference on Computational Natural Language Learning (CoNLL 2017), Vancouver, Canada, August 3-4, 2017*, pages 173–183.

Hannah Rashkin, Maarten Sap, Emily Allaway, Noah A. Smith, and Yejin Choi. 2018. Event2Mind: Commonsense inference on events, intents, and reactions. In *Proceedings of the 56th Annual Meeting of the Association for Computational Linguistics (Volume 1: Long Papers)*, pages 463–473, Melbourne, Australia. Association for Computational Linguistics.

Maarten Sap, Ronan Le Bras, Emily Allaway, Chandra Bhagavatula, Nicholas Lourie, Hannah Rashkin, Brendan Roof, Noah A. Smith, and Yejin Choi. 2019. ATOMIC: an atlas of machine commonsense for if-then reasoning. In *The Thirty-Third AAAI Conference on Artificial Intelligence*, pages 3027–3035.

Kailash Karthik Saravanakumar, Miguel Ballesteros, Muthu Kumar Chandrasekaran, and Kathleen McKeown. 2021. Event-driven news stream clustering using entity-aware contextual embeddings. In *Proceedings of the 16th Conference of the European Chapter of the Association for Computational Linguistics: Main Volume*, pages 2330–2340, Online. Association for Computational Linguistics.

Todor Staykovski, Alberto Barrón-Cedeno, Giovanni Da San Martino, and Preslav Nakov. 2019. Dense vs. sparse representations for news stream clustering. In *Text2Story@ ECIR*, pages 47–52.

Ananya Subburathinam, Di Lu, Heng Ji, Jonathan May, Shih-Fu Chang, Avirup Sil, and Clare Voss. 2019. Cross-lingual structure transfer for relation and event extraction. In *Proc. 2019 Conference on Empirical Methods in Natural Language Processing and 9th International Joint Conference on Natural Language Processing (EMNLP-IJCNLP2019)*.

Haoyu Wang, Muhao Chen, Hongming Zhang, and Dan Roth. 2020. Joint constrained learning for event-event relation extraction. In *Proceedings of the 2020 Conference on Empirical Methods in Natural Language Processing*. Association for Computational Linguistics.

Lu Wang, Claire Cardie, and Galen Marchetti. 2015. Socially-informed timeline generation for complex events. In *Proceedings of the 2015 Conference of the North American Chapter of the Association for Computational Linguistics: Human Language Technologies*, pages 1055–1065, Denver, Colorado. Association for Computational Linguistics.

Hui Yang, Tat-Seng Chua, Shuguang Wang, and Chun-Keat Koh. 2003. Structured use of external knowledge for event-based open domain question answering. In *Proceedings of the 26th annual international ACM SIGIR conference on Research and development in informaion retrieval*, pages 33–40.

Qi Zeng, Manling Li, Tuan Lai, Heng Ji, Mohit Bansal, and Hanghang Tong. 2021. Gene: Global event network embedding. In *Proc. NAACL-HLT2021 Workshop on Graph-Based Natural Language Processing*.

Hongming Zhang, Muhao Chen, Haoyu Wang, Yangqiu Song, and Dan Roth. 2020a. Open-domain process structure induction. In *Proceedings of the 2020 Conference on Empirical Methods in Natural Language Processing*. Association for Computational Linguistics.

Hongming Zhang, Daniel Khashabi, Yangqiu Song, and Dan Roth. 2020b. Transomcs: From linguistic graphs to commonsense knowledge. In *Proceedings of IJCAI 2020*, pages 4004–4010.

Hongming Zhang, Xin Liu, Haojie Pan, Yangqiu Song, and Cane Wing-Ki Leung. 2020c. ASER: A large-scale eventuality knowledge graph. In *WWW '20: The Web Conference 2020, Taipei, Taiwan, April 20-24, 2020*, pages 201–211.

Tianran Zhang, Muhao Chen, and Alex Bui. 2020d. Diagnostic prediction with sequence-of-sets representation learning for clinical event. In *Proceedings of the 18th International Conference on Artificial Intelligence in Medicine (AIME)*.

Zixuan Zhang and Heng Ji. 2021. Abstract meaning representation guided graph encoding and decoding for joint information extraction. In *Proc. The 2021 Conference of the North American Chapter of the Association for Computational Linguistics - Human Language Technologies (NAACL-HLT2021)*.

Ben Zhou, Qiang Ning, Daniel Khashabi, and Dan Roth. 2020. Temporal common sense acquisition with minimal supervision. In *Proceedings of the 58th Annual Meeting of the Association for Computational Linguistics*, pages 7579–7589, Online. Association for Computational Linguistics.

Cunchao Zhu, Muhao Chen, Changjun Fan, Guangquan Cheng, and Yan Zhan. 2021. Learning from history: Modeling temporal knowledge graphs with sequential copy-generation networks. In *Proceedings of the AAAI Conference on Artificial Intelligence (AAAI)*.

Meta Learning and Its Applications to Natural Language Processing

Hung-yi Lee
National Taiwan University
hungyilee@ntu.edu.tw

Ngoc Thang Vu
University of Stuttgart
thangvu@ims.uni-stuttgart.de

Shang-Wen Li
Amazon AI
shangwel@amazon.com

1 Brief Description

Deep learning based natural language processing (NLP) has become the mainstream of research in recent years and significantly outperforms conventional methods. However, deep learning models are notorious for being data and computation hungry. These downsides limit such models' application from deployment to different domains, languages, countries, or styles, since collecting in-genre data and model training from scratch are costly. The long-tail nature of human language makes challenges even more significant.

Meta-learning, or 'Learning to Learn', aims to learn better learning algorithms, including better parameter initialization, optimization strategy, network architecture, distance metrics, and beyond. Meta-learning has been shown to allow faster fine-tuning, converge to better performance, and achieve outstanding results for few-shot learning in many applications. Meta-learning is one of the most important new techniques in machine learning in recent years. There is a related tutorial in ICML 2019[1] and a related course at Stanford[2], but most of the example applications given in these materials are about image processing. It is believed that meta-learning has excellent potential to be applied in NLP, and some works have been proposed with notable achievements in several relevant problems, e.g., relation extraction, machine translation, and dialogue generation and state tracking. However, it does not catch the same level of attention as in the image processing community.

In the tutorial, we will first introduce Meta-learning approaches and the theory behind them, and then review the works of applying this technology to NLP problems. Table 1 summarizes the content this tutorial will cover. This tutorial intends to facilitate researchers in the NLP community to understand this new technology better and promote more research studies using this new technology.

2 Type of the tutorial

The type of tutorial is **Cutting-edge**. Meta-learning is a newly emerging topic. The area of natural language processing has seen a growing number of papers about Meta-learning. However, there is no tutorial systematically reviewing relevant works at ACL/EMNLP/NAACL/EACL/COLING.

3 Tutorial Structure and Content

A typical machine learning algorithm, e.g., deep learning, can be considered as a sophisticated function. The function takes training data as input and a trained model as output. Today the learning algorithms are mostly human-designed. These algorithms have already achieved significant progress towards artificial intelligence, but still far from optimal. Usually, these algorithms are designed for one specific task and need a lot of labeled training data. One possible method that could overcome these challenges is meta-learning, also known as 'Learning to Learn', which aims to learn the learning algorithm. In the image processing research community, meta-learning has shown to be successful, especially few-shot learning. It has recently also been widely adopted to a wide range of NLP applications, which usually suffer from data scarcity. This tutorial has two parts. In part I, we will introduce several meta-learning approaches (**estimated 1.5 hours**). In part II, we will highlight the applications of the meta-learning methods to NLP (**estimated 1.5 hours**).

3.1 Part I - Introduction of Meta Learning

We will start with the problem definition of meta-learning, and then introduce the most well-known meta-learning approaches below.

[1] https://sites.google.com/view/icml19metalearning

[2] http://cs330.stanford.edu/

Proceedings of the Joint Conference of the 59th Annual Meeting of the Association for Computational Linguistics and the 11th International Joint Conference on Natural Language Processing: Tutorial Abstracts, pages 15–20, August 1st, 2021.

Table 1: Referrence of NLP tasks using different meta-learning methods.

	(A) **Learning to initialize**	(B) **Learning to compare**	(C) **Other**
Text Classification	(Dou et al., 2019) (Bansal et al., 2019)	(Yu et al., 2018) (Tan et al., 2019) (Geng et al., 2019) (Sun et al., 2019)	Learning the learning algorithm: (Wu et al., 2019)
Sequence Labelng	(Wu et al., 2020)	(Hou et al., 2020)	
Machine Translation	(Gu et al., 2018) (Indurthi et al., 2020)		
Speech Recognition	(Hsu et al., 2020) (Klejch et al., 2019) (Winata et al., 2020a) (Winata et al., 2020b)		Learning to optimize: (Klejch et al., 2018) Network architecture search: (Chen et al., 2020b) (Baruwa et al., 2019)
Relation Classification	(Obamuyide and Vlachos, 2019) (Bose et al., 2019) (Lv et al., 2019) (Wang et al., 2019)	(Ye and Ling, 2019) (Chen et al., 2019a) (Xiong et al., 2018) (Gao et al., 2019)	
Dialogue	(Qian and Yu, 2019) (Madotto et al., 2019) (Mi et al., 2019)		Learning to optimize: (Chien and Lieow, 2019)
Parsing	(Guo et al., 2019) (Huang et al., 2018)		
Word Embedding	(Hu et al., 2019)	(Sun et al., 2018)	
Multi-model		(Eloff et al., 2019)	Learning the learning algorithm: (Surís et al., 2019)
Keyword Spotting	(Chen et al., 2020a)		Network architecture search: (Mazzawi et al., 2019)
Sound Event Detection		(Shimada et al., 2020) (Chou et al., 2019)	
Voice Cloning			Learning the learning algorithm: (Chen et al., 2019b) (Serrà et al., 2019)

3.1.1 Learning to Initialize

Gradient descent is the core learning algorithm for deep learning. Most of the components in gradient descent are handcrafted. First, we have to determine how to initialize network parameters. Then the gradient is computed to update the parameters, and the learning rates are determined heuristically. Determining these components usually need experience, intuition, and trial and error. With meta-learning, those hyperparameters can be learned from data automatically. Among these series of approaches, learning a set of parameters to initialize gradient descent, or learning to initialize, is already widely studied.

Column (A) of Table 1 lists the NLP papers using learning to initialize. Learning to initialize is the most widely applied meta-learning approach in NLP today. The idea of learning to initialize spreads quickly in NLP probably because the idea of looking for better initialization is already widespread before the development of meta-learning. The researchers of NLP have applied lots of different transfer learning techniques to find a set of good initialization parameters for a specific task from its related tasks. Here we will not only introduce learning to initialize but also compare its difference with typical transfer learning.

3.1.2 Learning to Compare

Besides the gradient descent-based learning algorithm, the testing examples' labels are determined by their similarity to the training examples in some learning algorithms. In this category, methods to compute the distance between two data points are crucial. Therefore, a series of approaches have been proposed to learn the distance measures for the learning algorithms. This category of approaches is also known as metric-based approaches.

Column (B) of Table 1 lists the NLP papers using learning to compare. Natural language is intrinsically represented as sophisticated sequences. Comparing the similarity of two sequences is not trivial, and widely used handcrafted measures, such as, Euclidean distance, cannot be directly applied, which motivates the research of learning to compare in NLP.

3.1.3 Other Methods

Although the above two methods dominate the NLP field at the moment, other meta-learning approaches have also shown their potential. For example, besides parameter initialization, other gradient descent components such as learning rates and network structures can also be learned. In addition to learning the components in the existing learning algorithm, some attempts even make the machine invent an entirely new learning algorithm beyond gradient descent. There is already some effort towards learning a function that directly takes training data as input and outputs network parameters for the target task. Column (C) of Table 1 lists these methods.

3.2 Part II - Applications to NLP tasks

There is a growing number of studies applying meta-learning techniques to NLP applications and achieving excellent results. In the second part of the tutorial, we will review these studies. Here we summarize these studies by categorizing their applications. Please refer to Table 1 for a detailed list of studies we plan to cover in the tutorial.

3.2.1 Text Classification

Text classification has a vast spectrum of applications, such as sentiment classification and intent classification. The meta-learning algorithms developed for image classification can be applied to text classification with slight modification to incorporate domain knowledge in each application (Yu et al., 2018; Tan et al., 2019; Geng et al., 2019; Sun et al., 2019; Dou et al., 2019; Bansal et al., 2019).

3.2.2 Sequence Labeling

Using a meta-learning algorithm to make the model fast adapt to new languages or domains is also useful for sequence labeling like name-entity recognition (NER) (Wu et al., 2020) and slot tagging (Hou et al., 2020). However, the typical meta-learning methods developed on image classification may not be optimal for sequence labeling because sequence labeling benefits from modeling the dependencies between labels, which is not leveraged in typical meta-learning methods. Techniques, such as the collapsing labeling mechanism, are proposed to optimize meta-learning for sequence labeling problem (Hou et al., 2020).

3.2.3 Automatic Speech Recognition and Neural Machine Translation

Automatic speech recognition (ASR), Neural machine translation (NMT), and speech translation require a large amount of labeled training data. Collecting such data is cost-prohibitive. To facilitate the expansion of such systems to new use cases, meta-learning is applied in these systems for the fast adaptation to new languages in NMT (Gu et al., 2018) and ASR (Hsu et al., 2020; Chen et al., 2020b), and fast adaptation to new accents (Winata et al., 2020b), new speakers (Klejch et al., 2019, 2018), code-switching (Winata et al., 2020a) in ASR.

3.2.4 Relation Classification and Knowledge Graph Completion

The typical supervised learning approaches for relation classification and link prediction for knowledge graph completion require a large number of training instances for each relation. However, only about 10% of relations in Wikidata have no more than ten triples (Vrandei and Krtzsch, 2014), so many long-tail relations suffer from data sparsity. Therefore, meta-learning has been applied to the relation classification and knowledge graph completion to improve the performance of the relations with limited training examples (Obamuyide and Vlachos, 2019; Bose et al., 2019; Lv et al., 2019; Wang et al., 2019; Ye and Ling, 2019; Chen et al., 2019a; Xiong et al., 2018; Gao et al., 2019).

3.2.5 Task-oriented Dialogue and Chatbot

Domain adaptation is an essential task in dialog system building because modern personal assistants, such as Alexa and Siri, are composed of thousands of single-domain task-oriented dialog systems. However, training a learnable model for a task requires a large amount of labeled in-domain data, and collecting and annotating training data for the tasks is costly since it involves real user interactions. Therefore, researchers apply meta-learning to learn from multiple rich-resource tasks and adapt the meta-learned models to new domains with minimal training samples for dialog response generation (Qian and Yu, 2019) and dialogue state tracking (DST) (Huang et al., 2020).

Also, training personalized chatbot that can mimic speakers with different personas is useful but challenging. Collecting many dialogs involving a specific persona is expensive, while it is challenging to capture a persona using only a few conversations. Thus, meta-learning comes into play for learning persona with few-shot example conversations (Madotto et al., 2019).

4 Diversity

As the main applications of the meta-learning approaches are to find better metrics, model architectures, or initializations such that the meta-trained model can generalize well in new tasks with limited data, the approach is often used at efficient knowledge transferring between domains and languages, and has seen many promising results. Meta-learning has the potential to democratize the progress of machine learning and NLP for different domains, languages, and countries in a scalable way.

5 Prerequisites for the attendees

The attendees have to understand derivatives as found in introductory Calculus and understand basic machine learning concepts such as classification, model optimization, and gradient descent.

6 Reading list

We encourage the audience to read the papers of some well-known meta-learning techqnieus before the tutorial, which are listed below.

- Learning to Initialize (Finn et al., 2017)
- Learning to Compare (Snell et al., 2017; Vinyals et al., 2016)
- Other Methods (Ravi and Larochelle, 2017; Andrychowicz et al., 2016)

7 Biographies of Presenters

Hung-yi Lee[3] received the M.S. and Ph.D. degrees from National Taiwan University (NTU), Taipei, Taiwan, in 2010 and 2012, respectively. From September 2012 to August 2013, he was a postdoctoral fellow in Research Center for Information Technology Innovation, Academia Sinica. From September 2013 to July 2014, he was a visiting scientist at the Spoken Language Systems Group of MIT Computer Science and Artificial Intelligence Laboratory (CSAIL). He is currently an associate professor of the Department of Electrical Engineering of National Taiwan University, with a joint appointment at the Department of Computer Science Information Engineering of the university. His research focuses on machine learning (especially deep learning), speech processing and natural language processing. He owns a YouTube channel teaching deep learning (in Mandarin) with more than **5M** views and **60k** subscribers.

Ngoc Thang Vu[4] received his Diploma (2009) and PhD (2014) degrees in computer science from Karlsruhe Institute of Technology, Germany. From 2014 to 2015, he worked at Nuance Communications as a senior research scientist and at Ludwig-Maximilian University Munich as an acting professor in computational linguistics. In 2015, he was appointed assistant professor at University of Stuttgart, Germany. Since 2018, he has been a full professor at the Institute for Natural Language Processing in Stuttgart. His main research interests are natural language processing (esp. speech recognition and dialog systems) and machine learning (esp. deep learning) for low-resource settings.

Shang-Wen Li[5] is a senior Applied Scientist at Amazon AI. His research focuses on spoken language understanding, dialog management, and natural language generation. His recent interest is transfer learning for low-resourced conversational bots. He earned his Ph.D. from MIT Computer Science and Artificial Intelligence Laboratory (CSAIL) in 2016. He received M.S. and B.S. from National Taiwan University. Before joining Amazon, he also worked at Apple Siri researching conversational AI.

8 Open access

We will allow the publication of our slides and video recording of the tutorial in the ACL Anthology.

References

Marcin Andrychowicz, Misha Denil, Sergio Gomez, Matthew W. Hoffman, David Pfau, Tom Schaul, Brendan Shillingford, and Nando de Freitas. 2016. Learning to learn by gradient descent by gradient descent. In *NIPS*.

Trapit Bansal, Rishikesh Jha, and Andrew McCallum. 2019. Learning to few-shot learn across diverse natural language classification tasks. In *arXiv*.

Ahmed Baruwa, Mojeed Abisiga, Ibrahim Gbadegesin, and Afeez Fakunle. 2019. Leveraging end-to-end speech recognition with neural architecture search. In *IJSER*.

Avishek Joey Bose, Ankit Jain, Piero Molino, and William L. Hamilton. 2019. Meta-graph:few shot link prediction via meta learning. In *arXiv*.

Mingyang Chen, Wen Zhang, Wei Zhang, Qiang Chen, and Huajun Chen. 2019a. Meta relational learning for few-shot link prediction in knowledge graphs. In *EMNLP*.

Yangbin Chen, Tom Ko, Lifeng Shang, Xiao Chen, Xin Jiang, and Qing Li. 2020a. An investigation of few-shot learning in spoken term classification. In *INTERSPEECH*.

Yi-Chen Chen, Jui-Yang Hsu, Cheng-Kuang Lee, and Hung yi Lee. 2020b. DARTS-ASR: Differentiable architecture search for multilingual speech recognition and adaptation. In *INTERSPEECH*.

[3]`https://speech.ee.ntu.edu.tw/~hylee/index.html`

[4]`https://www.ims.uni-stuttgart.de/en/institute/team/Vu-00002`

[5]`https://scholar.google.com/citations?user=wFI97HUAAAAJ`

Yutian Chen, Yannis Assael, Brendan Shillingford, David Budden, Scott Reed, Heiga Zen, Quan Wang, Luis C. Cobo, Andrew Trask, Ben Laurie, Caglar Gulcehre, Aäron van den Oord, Oriol Vinyals, and Nando de Freitas. 2019b. Sample efficient adaptive text-to-speech. In *ICLR*.

Jen-Tzung Chien and Wei Xiang Lieow. 2019. Meta learning for hyperparameter optimization in dialogue system. In *INTERSPEECH*.

Szu-Yu Chou, Kai-Hsiang Cheng, Jyh-Shing Roger Jang, and Yi-Hsuan Yang. 2019. Learning to match transient sound events using attentional similarity for few-shot sound recognition. In *ICASSP*.

Zi-Yi Dou, Keyi Yu, and Antonios Anastasopoulos. 2019. Investigating meta-learning algorithms for low-resource natural language understanding tasks. In *EMNLP*.

Ryan Eloff, Herman A. Engelbrecht, and Herman Kamper. 2019. Multimodal one-shot learning of speech and images. In *ICASSP*.

Chelsea Finn, Pieter Abbeel, and Sergey Levine. 2017. Model-agnostic meta-learning for fast adaptation of deep networks. In *ICML*.

Tianyu Gao, Xu Han, Zhiyuan Liu, and Maosong Sun. 2019. Hybrid attention-based prototypical networks for noisy few-shot relation classification. In *AAAI*.

Ruiying Geng, Binhua Li, Yongbin Li, Xiaodan Zhu, Ping Jian, and Jian Sun. 2019. Induction networks for few-shot text classification. In *EMNLP*.

Jiatao Gu, Yong Wang, Yun Chen, Kyunghyun Cho, and Victor O.K. Li. 2018. Meta-learning for low-resource neural machine translation. In *EMNLP*.

Daya Guo, Duyu Tang, Nan Duan, Ming Zhou, and Jian Yin. 2019. Coupling retrieval and meta-learning for context-dependent semantic parsing. In *ACL*.

Yutai Hou, Wanxiang Che, Yongkui Lai, Zhihan Zhou, Yijia Liu, Han Liu, and Ting Liu. 2020. Few-shot slot tagging with collapsed dependency transfer and label-enhanced task-adaptive projection network. In *ACL*.

Jui-Yang Hsu, Yuan-Jui Chen, and Hung yi Lee. 2020. Meta learning for end-to-end low-resource speech recognition. In *ICASSP*.

Ziniu Hu, Ting Chen, Kai-Wei Chang, and Yizhou Sun. 2019. Few-shot representation learning for out-of-vocabulary words. In *ACL*.

Po-Sen Huang, Chenglong Wang, Rishabh Singh, Wen tau Yih, and Xiaodong He. 2018. Natural language to structured query generation via meta-learning. In *NAACL*.

Yi Huang, Junlan Feng, Min Hu, Xiaoting Wu, Xiaoyu Du, and Shuo Ma. 2020. Meta-reinforced multi-domain state generator for dialogue systems. In *ACL*.

Sathish Indurthi, Houjeung Han, Nikhil Kumar Lakumarapu, Beomseok Lee, Insoo Chung, Sangha Kim, and Chanwoo Kim. 2020. Data efficient direct speech-to-text translation with modality agnostic meta-learning. In *ICASSP*.

Ondřej Klejch, Joachim Fainberg, and Peter Bell. 2018. Learning to adapt:a meta-learning approach for speaker adaptation. In *INTERSPEECH*.

Ondřej Klejch, Joachim Fainberg, Peter Bell, and Steve Renals. 2019. Speaker adaptive training using model agnostic meta-learning. In *ASRU*.

Xin Lv, Yuxian Gu, Xu Han, Lei Hou, Juanzi Li, and Zhiyuan Liu. 2019. Adapting meta knowledge graph information for multi-hop reasoning over few-shot relations. In *EMNLP*.

Andrea Madotto, Zhaojiang Lin, Chien-Sheng Wu, and Pascale Fung. 2019. Personalizing dialogue agents via meta-learning. In *ACL*.

Hanna Mazzawi, Xavi Gonzalvo, Aleks Kracun, Prashant Sridhar, Niranjan Subrahmanya, Ignacio Lopez Moreno, Hyun Jin Park, and Patrick Violette. 2019. Improving keyword spotting and language identification via neural architecture search at scale. In *INTERSPEECH*.

Fei Mi, Minlie Huang, Jiyong Zhang, and Boi Faltings. 2019. Meta-learning for low-resource natural language generation in task-oriented dialogue systems. In *IJCAI*.

Abiola Obamuyide and Andreas Vlachos. 2019. Model-agnostic meta-learning for relation classification with limited supervision. In *ACL*.

Kun Qian and Zhou Yu. 2019. Domain adaptive dialog generation via meta learning. In *ACL*.

Sachin Ravi and Hugo Larochelle. 2017. Optimization as a model for few-shot learning. In *ICLR*.

Joan Serrà, Santiago Pascual, and Carlos Segura. 2019. Blow:a single-scale hyperconditioned flow for non-parallel raw-audio voice conversion. In *NeurIPS*.

Kazuki Shimada, Yuichiro Koyama, and Akira Inoue. 2020. Metric learning with background noise class for few-shot detection of rare sound events. In *ICASSP*.

Jake Snell, Kevin Swersky, and Richard S. Zemel. 2017. Prototypical networks for few-shot learning. In *NIPS*.

Jingyuan Sun, Shaonan Wang, and Chengqing Zong. 2018. Memory, show the way:memory based few shot word representation learning. In *EMNLP*.

Shengli Sun, Qingfeng Sun, Kevin Zhou, and Tengchao Lv. 2019. Hierarchical attention prototypical networks for few-shot text classification. In *EMNLP*.

Dídac Surís, Dave Epstein, Heng Ji, Shih-Fu Chang, and Carl Vondrick. 2019. Learning to learn words from narrated video. In *arXiv*.

Ming Tan, Yang Yu, Haoyu Wang, Dakuo Wang, Saloni Potdar, Shiyu Chang, and Mo Yu. 2019. Out-of-domain detection for low-resource text classification tasks. In *EMNLP*.

Oriol Vinyals, Charles Blundell, Timothy Lillicrap, Koray Kavukcuoglu, and Daan Wierstra. 2016. Matching networks for one shot learning. In *NIPS*.

Denny Vrandei and Markus Krtzsch. 2014. Wikidata: A free collaborative knowledge base. In *Communications of the ACM*.

Zihao Wang, Kwun Ping Lai, Piji Li, Lidong Bing, and Wai Lam. 2019. Tackling long-tailed relations and uncommon entities in knowledge graph completion. In *EMNLP*.

Genta Indra Winata, Samuel Cahyawijaya, Zhaojiang Lin, Zihan Liu, Peng Xu, and Pascale Fung. 2020a. Meta-transfer learning for code-switched speech recognition. In *ACL*.

Genta Indra Winata, Samuel Cahyawijaya, Zihan Liu, Zhaojiang Lin, Andrea Madotto, Peng Xu, and Pascale Fung. 2020b. Learning fast adaptation on cross-accented speech recognition. In *INTERSPEECH*.

Jiawei Wu, Wenhan Xiong, and William Yang Wang. 2019. Learning to learn and predict: A meta-learning approach for multi-label classification. In *EMNLP*.

Qianhui Wu, Zijia Lin, Guoxin Wang, Hui Chen, Börje F. Karlsson, Biqing Huang, and Chin-Yew Lin. 2020. Enhanced meta-learning for cross-lingual named entity recognition with minimal resources. In *AAAI*.

Wenhan Xiong, Mo Yu, Shiyu Chang, Xiaoxiao Guo, and William Yang Wang. 2018. One-shot relational learning for knowledge graphs. In *EMNLP*.

Zhi-Xiu Ye and Zhen-Hua Ling. 2019. Multi-level matching and aggregation network for few-shot relation classification. In *ACL*.

Mo Yu, Xiaoxiao Guo, Jinfeng Yi, Shiyu Chang, Saloni Potdar, Yu Cheng, Gerald Tesauro, Haoyu Wang, and Bowen Zhou. 2018. Diverse few-shot text classification with multiple metrics. In *ACL*.

Pre-training Methods for Neural Machine Translation

Mingxuan Wang
ByteDance AI Lab
wangmingxuan.89@bytedance.com

Lei Li
ByteDance AI Lab
lileilab@bytedance.com

1 Tutorial Introduction

Pre-training is a dominant paradigm in Nature Language Processing (NLP) (Radford et al., 2019; Devlin et al., 2019; Liu et al., 2019a), Computer Vision (CV) (He et al., 2019; Xie et al., 2020) and Auto Speech Recognition (ASR) (Bansal et al., 2019; Chuang et al., 2020; Park et al., 2019). Typically, the models are first pre-trained on large amount of unlabeled data to capture rich representations of the input, and then applied to the downstream tasks by either providing context-aware representation of the input, or initializing the parameters of the downstream model for fine-tuning. Recently, the trend of self-supervised pre-training and task-specific fine-tuning finally fully hits neural machine translation (NMT) (Zhu et al., 2020; Yang et al., 2020; Chen et al., 2020).

Despite its success, introducing a universal pre-trained model to NMT is non-trivial and not necessarily yields promising results, especially for the resource-rich setup. Unique challenges remain in several aspects. First, the objective of most pre-training methods are different from the downstream NMT tasks. For example, BERT (Devlin et al., 2019), a popular pre-trained model, is designed for language understanding with only a transformer encoder, while an NMT model usually consists of an encoder and a decoder to perform cross-lingual generation. This gap makes it not feasible enough to apply pre-training for NMT (Song et al., 2019). Besides, machine translation is naturally a multi-lingual problem, but general pre-training methods for NLP mainly focus on English corpus, such as BERT and GPT. Given the success of transfer learning in multi-lingual machine translation, it is very appealing to introduce multi-lingual pre-training for NMT (Conneau and Lample, 2019). Finally, speech translation has attracted much attention recently, while most pre-training methods are focused on text representation. How to leverage the pre-training methods to improve the speech translation becomes a new challenge.

This tutorial provides a comprehensive guide to make the most of pre-training for neural machine translation. Firstly, we will briefly introduce the background of NMT, pre-training methodology, and point out the main challenges when applying pre-training for NMT. Then we will focus on analysing the role of pre-training in enhancing the performance of NMT, how to design a better pre-training model for executing specific NMT tasks and how to better integrate the pre-trained model into NMT system. In each part, we will provide examples, discuss training techniques and analyse what is transferred when applying pre-training.

The first topic is the *monolingual pre-training for NMT*, which is one of the most well-studied field. Monolingual text representations like ELMo, GPT, MASS and BERT have superiorities, which significantly boost the performances of various natural language processing tasks (Peters et al., 2018; Devlin et al., 2019; Radford et al., 2019; Song et al., 2019). However, NMT has several distinct characteristics, such as the availability of large training data (10 million or larger) and the high capacity of baseline NMT models, which requires carefully design of pre-training. In this part, we will introduce different pre-training methods and analyse the best practice when applying them to different machine translation scenarios, such as unsupervised NMT, low-resource NMT and rich-source NMT (Zhu et al., 2020; Yang et al., 2020). We will cover techniques to finetune the pre-trained models with various strategies, such as knowledge distillation and adapter (Bapna and Firat, 2019; Liang et al., 2021).

The next topic is *multi-lingual pre-training for NMT*. In this context, we aims at mitigating the English-centric bias and suggest that it is possible

Proceedings of the Joint Conference of the 59th Annual Meeting of the Association for Computational Linguistics and the 11th International Joint Conference on Natural Language Processing: Tutorial Abstracts, pages 21–25, August 1st, 2021.

to build universal representation for different language to improve massive multi-lingual NMT. In this part, we will discuss the general representation of different languages and analyse how knowledge transfers across languages. These will allow a better design for multi-lingual pre-training, in particular for zero-shot transfer to non-English language pairs (Johnson et al., 2017; Qi et al., 2018; Conneau and Lample, 2019; Pires et al., 2019; Huang et al., 2019; Lin et al., 2020; Liu et al., 2020; Pan et al., 2021; Lin et al., 2021).

The last technical part of this tutorial deals with the *Pre-training for speech NMT*. In particular, we focus on leverage weakly supervised or unsupervised training data to improve speech translation. In this part, we will discuss the possibilities of building a general representations across speech and text. And shows how text or audio pre-training can guild the text generation of NMT (Wang et al., 2019; Liu et al., 2019b; Bansal et al., 2019; Wang et al., 2020; Baevski et al., 2020a,b; Huang et al., 2021; Long et al., 2021; Dong et al., 2021b,a; Han et al., 2021; Ye et al., 2021).

We conclude the tutorial by pointing out the best practice when applying pre-training for NMT. The topics cover various of pre-training methods for different NMT scenarios. After this tutorial, the audience will understand why pre-training for NMT is different from other tasks and how to make the most of pre-training for NMT. Importantly, we will give deep analyze about how and why pre-training works in NMT, which will inspire future work on designing pre-training paradigm specific for NMT.

2 Tutorial Outline

PART I: Introduction (15 min)

- Background of NMT
- General pre-training paradigm
- Unique Challenges
  - Objective difference
  - Multi-lingual generation
  - Modality disparity

PART II: Monolingual Pre-training for NMT (60 min)

- The early stage
  - NMT initialized with word2vec
  - NMT initialized with language model
- BERT fusion in NMT
  - BERT Incorporating methods
  - BERT Tuning methods
- Unified sequence-to-sequence pre-training
  - MASS, Bart, etc.

PART III: Multi-lingual Pre-training for NMT (45 min)

- Multilingual fused pre-training
  - Cross-lingual Language Model Pre-training
  - Alternating Language Modeling Pre-training
  - XLM-T: Cross-lingual Transformer Encoders
- Multilingual sequence to sequence pre-training
  - mBART
  - CSP
  - mRASP

PART IV: Pre-training for Speech Translation (45 min)

- MT pre-training
- ASR pre-training
- Audio pre-training
- Raw text pre-training
- Bi-modal pre-training

PART V: Conclusion and Future Directions (15 min)

3 Type of Tutorial

Cutting-edge. In this tutorial, we will discuss the most advanced techniques of pre-training for neural machine translation. The instructors will also present their own practical experiences in enhancing a machine translation service as a product, which are usually not found in papers.

4 Tutorial Breadth

Based on the representative set of papers listed in the selected bibliography, we anticipate that 70%-80% of the tutorial will cover other researchers' work, while the rest concerns the work where at least one of the presenters has been actively involved in. We will introduce several important work related to the monolingual, the multi-lingual and the multi-modal pre-training for NMT.

5 Diversity

In the tutorial, some multilingual pre-training methods will scale to over 50 to 100 different languages. Researchers working on the diverse language pairs might find this tutorial relevant and useful.

6 Prerequisites

The tutorial is self-contained. We will address the background, the technical details and the examples. Basic knowledge about neural networks are required, including word embeddings, attention, and encoder-decoder models. Prior NLP courses and familiarity with the machine translation task are preferred.

It is recommended (and optional) that audience to read the following papers before the tutorial:

1. Basic MT model: Attention is all you need (Vaswani et al., 2017).
2. Google's multilingual neural machine translation system (Johnson et al., 2017).
3. Text pre-training with BERT (Devlin et al., 2019) and GPT (Radford et al., 2019).
4. Audio pre-training with Wav2vec and Wav2vec2.0 (Schneider et al., 2019; Baevski et al., 2020b).
5. Pre-training multilingual NMT (Lin et al., 2020; Liu et al., 2020).

7 Target Audience

This tutorial will be suitable for researchers and practitioners interested in pre-training applications and multilingual NLP, especially for machine translation.

To the best of our knowledge, this is the first tutorial that focuses on the pre-training methods and practice for NMT.

8 Technical Requirements

The tutorial will be online. Internet connection with proper live video device is needed.

9 Open access

Our slides and video is open to public, available at `https://lileicc.github.io/TALKS/2021-ACL/`.

10 Tutorial Presenters

Mingxuan Wang (ByteDance AI Lab)
Google Scholar

Dr. Mingxuan Wang is a senior researcher at ByteDance AI Lab. He received his PhD degree from the Chinese Academy of Sciences Institute of Computing Technology in 2017. His research focuses on natural language processing and machine translation. He has published over 20 papers in leading NLP/AI journals and conferences such as ACL, AAAI and EMNLP. He has served in the Program Committee for ACL/EMNLP 2016-2020, AAAI/IJCAI 2018/2019, NeurIPS 2020. He achieved outstanding results in various machine translation evaluation competitions, including the first place of Chinese-to-English translation at at the WMT 2018, the third place of Chinese-to-English translation at NIST 2015, etc. Together with Dr. Lei Li, he is leading a team developing the VolcTrans machine translation system.

He has given a tutorial about Machine Translation at CCMT 2017 and was an guest lecturer for 2016 Machine Translation for University of Chinese Academy of Sciences (UCAS).

Lei Li (ByteDance AI Lab)
https://lileicc.github.io/

Dr. Lei Li is Director of ByteDance AI Lab, leading the research and product development for NLP, robotics, and drug discovery. His research interests are machine translation, speech translation, text generation, and AI powered drug discovery. He received his B.S. from Shanghai Jiao Tong University and Ph.D. from Carnegie Mellon University, respectively. His dissertation work on fast algorithms for mining co-evolving time series was awarded ACM KDD best dissertation (runner up). His recent work on AI writer Xiaomingbot received 2nd-class award of Wu Wen-tsün AI prize in 2017. He is a recipient of CCF distinguished speaker in 2017, and CCF Young Elite award in 2019. His team won first places for five language translation directions in WMT 2020 and the best in corpus filtering challenge. Before ByteDance, he worked at EECS department of UC Berkeley and Baidu's Institute of Deep Learning in Silicon Valley. He has served organizers and area chair/senior PC for multiple conferences including KDD, EMNLP, NeurIPS, AAAI, IJCAI, and CIKM. He has published over 100 technical papers in ML, NLP and data mining and holds more than 10 patents. He has started and is developing ByteDance's machine translation system, VolcTrans and many of his algorithms have been deployed.

He has delivered four tutorials at EMNLP 2019, NLPCC 2019, NLPCC 2016, and KDD 2010. He was an lecturer for 2014 Probabilistic Programming for Advancing Machine Learning summer school at Portland, USA.

11 Other Information

Prior Related Tutorials Neural Machine Translation, presented by Thang Luong, Kyunghyun Cho, and Christopher Manning at ACL 2016. This tutorial is related but different from ACL 2016 NMT tutorial. It focuses on pre-training methods for both bilingual, multi-lingual, and multi-modal neural machine translation.

Unsupervised Cross-Lingual Representation Learning, presented by Sebastian Ruder, Anders Søgaard, and Ivan Vulić at ACL 2019. This tutorial is related in concerning multi-lingual NLP. However, their tutorial was on representation learning, while our tutorial is on neural machine translation.

References

Alexei Baevski, Steffen Schneider, and Michael Auli. 2020a. vq-wav2vec: Self-supervised learning of discrete speech representations. In *Proc. of ICLR*.

Alexei Baevski, Yuhao Zhou, Abdelrahman Mohamed, and Michael Auli. 2020b. wav2vec 2.0: A framework for self-supervised learning of speech representations. In *Proc. of NeurIPS*.

Sameer Bansal, Herman Kamper, Karen Livescu, Adam Lopez, and Sharon Goldwater. 2019. Pre-training on high-resource speech recognition improves low-resource speech-to-text translation. In *Proc. of NAACL-HLT*, pages 58–68.

Ankur Bapna and Orhan Firat. 2019. Simple, scalable adaptation for neural machine translation. In *Proc. of EMNLP*, pages 1538–1548.

Yen-Chun Chen, Zhe Gan, Yu Cheng, Jingzhou Liu, and Jingjing Liu. 2020. Distilling knowledge learned in BERT for text generation. In *Proc. of ACL*, pages 7893–7905.

Yung-Sung Chuang, Chi-Liang Liu, and Hung-Yi Lee. 2020. SpeechBERT: An audio-and-text jointly learned language model for end-to-end spoken question answering. In *Proc. of INTERSPEECH*.

Alexis Conneau and Guillaume Lample. 2019. Cross-lingual language model pretraining. In *Proc. of NeurIPS*, pages 7057–7067.

Jacob Devlin, Ming-Wei Chang, Kenton Lee, and Kristina Toutanova. 2019. BERT: Pre-training of deep bidirectional transformers for language understanding. In *Proc. of NAACL-HLT*, pages 4171–4186.

Qianqian Dong, Mingxuan Wang, Hao Zhou, Shuang Xu, Bo Xu, and Lei Li. 2021a. Consecutive decoding for speech-to-text translation. In *Proc. of AAAI*.

Qianqian Dong, Rong Ye, Mingxuan Wang, Hao Zhou, Shuang Xu, Bo Xu, and Lei Li. 2021b. Listen, understand and translate: Triple supervision decouples end-to-end speech-to-text translation. In *Proc. of AAAI*, volume 35, pages 12749–12759.

Chi Han, Mingxuan Wang, Heng Ji, and Lei Li. 2021. Learning shared semantic space for speech-to-text translation. In *Proc. of ACL - Findings*.

Kaiming He, Ross B. Girshick, and Piotr Dollár. 2019. Rethinking imagenet pre-training. In *Proc. of ICCV*, pages 4917–4926.

Haoyang Huang, Yaobo Liang, Nan Duan, Ming Gong, Linjun Shou, Daxin Jiang, and Ming Zhou. 2019. Unicoder: A universal language encoder by pre-training with multiple cross-lingual tasks. In *Proc. of EMNLP*, pages 2485–2494.

Haoyang Huang, Lin Su, Di Qi, Nan Duan, Edward Cui, Taroon Bharti, Lei Zhang, Lijuan Wang, Jianfeng Gao, Bei Liu, et al. 2021. M3p: Learning universal representations via multitask multilingual multimodal pre-training. In *Proc. of CVPR*.

Melvin Johnson, Mike Schuster, Quoc V. Le, Maxim Krikun, Yonghui Wu, Zhifeng Chen, Nikhil Thorat, Fernanda Viégas, Martin Wattenberg, Greg Corrado, Macduff Hughes, and Jeffrey Dean. 2017. Google's multilingual neural machine translation system: Enabling zero-shot translation. *TACL*, 5:339–351.

Jianze Liang, Chengqi Zhao, Mingxuan Wang, Xipeng Qiu, and Lei Li. 2021. Finding sparse structure for domain specific neural machine translation. In *Proc. of AAAI*.

Zehui Lin, Xiao Pan, Mingxuan Wang, Xipeng Qiu, Jiangtao Feng, Hao Zhou, and Lei Li. 2020. Pre-training multilingual neural machine translation by leveraging alignment information. In *Proc. of EMNLP*, pages 2649–2663.

Zehui Lin, Liwei Wu, Mingxuan Wang, and Lei Li. 2021. Learning language specific sub-network for multilingual machine translation. In *Proc. of ACL*.

Yinhan Liu, Jiatao Gu, Naman Goyal, Xian Li, Sergey Edunov, Marjan Ghazvininejad, Mike Lewis, and Luke Zettlemoyer. 2020. Multilingual denoising pre-training for neural machine translation. *TACL*, 8:726–742.

Yinhan Liu, Myle Ott, Naman Goyal, Jingfei Du, Mandar Joshi, Danqi Chen, Omer Levy, Mike Lewis, Luke S. Zettlemoyer, and Veselin Stoyanov. 2019a. Roberta: A robustly optimized bert pretraining approach. *ArXiv*, abs/1907.11692.

Yuchen Liu, Hao Xiong, Jiajun Zhang, Zhongjun He, Hua Wu, Haifeng Wang, and Chengqing Zong. 2019b. End-to-end speech translation with knowledge distillation. In *Proc. of INTERSPEECH*, pages 1128–1132.

Quanyu Long, Mingxuan Wang, and Lei Li. 2021. Generative imagination elevates machine translation. In *Proc. of NAACL-HLT*, pages 5738–5748.

Xiao Pan, Liwei Wu, Mingxuan Wang, and Lei Li. 2021. Contrastive learning for many-to-many multilingual neural machine translation. In *Proc. of ACL*.

Daniel S Park, William Chan, Yu Zhang, Chung-Cheng Chiu, Barret Zoph, Ekin D Cubuk, and Quoc V Le. 2019. Specaugment: A simple data augmentation method for automatic speech recognition. In *Proc. of INTERSPEECH*.

Matthew Peters, Mark Neumann, Mohit Iyyer, Matt Gardner, Christopher Clark, Kenton Lee, and Luke Zettlemoyer. 2018. Deep contextualized word representations. In *Proc. of NAACL-HLT*, pages 2227–2237.

Telmo Pires, Eva Schlinger, and Dan Garrette. 2019. How multilingual is multilingual BERT? In *Proc. of ACL*, pages 4996–5001.

Ye Qi, Devendra Sachan, Matthieu Felix, Sarguna Padmanabhan, and Graham Neubig. 2018. When and why are pre-trained word embeddings useful for neural machine translation? In *Proc. of NAACL-HLT*, pages 529–535.

Alec Radford, Jeffrey Wu, Rewon Child, David Luan, Dario Amodei, and Ilya Sutskever. 2019. Language models are unsupervised multitask learners. *OpenAI Blog*, 1(8).

Steffen Schneider, Alexei Baevski, Ronan Collobert, and Michael Auli. 2019. wav2vec: Unsupervised pre-training for speech recognition. In *Proc. of INTERSPEECH*.

Kaitao Song, Xu Tan, Tao Qin, Jianfeng Lu, and Tie-Yan Liu. 2019. MASS: masked sequence to sequence pre-training for language generation. In *Proc. of ICML*, volume 97 of *Proceedings of Machine Learning Research*, pages 5926–5936.

Ashish Vaswani, Noam Shazeer, Niki Parmar, Jakob Uszkoreit, Llion Jones, Aidan N. Gomez, Lukasz Kaiser, and Illia Polosukhin. 2017. Attention is all you need. In *Proc. of NeurIPS*, pages 5998–6008.

Chengyi Wang, Yu Wu, Shujie Liu, Ming Zhou, and Zhenglu Yang. 2020. Curriculum pre-training for end-to-end speech translation. In *Proc. of ACL*, pages 3728–3738.

Xin Wang, Jiawei Wu, Junkun Chen, Lei Li, Yuan-Fang Wang, and William Yang Wang. 2019. Vatex: A large-scale, high-quality multilingual dataset for video-and-language research. In *Proc. of ICCV*, pages 4580–4590.

Qizhe Xie, Minh-Thang Luong, Eduard H. Hovy, and Quoc V. Le. 2020. Self-training with noisy student improves imagenet classification. In *Proc. of CVPR*, pages 10684–10695.

Jiacheng Yang, Mingxuan Wang, Hao Zhou, Chengqi Zhao, Weinan Zhang, Yong Yu, and Lei Li. 2020. Towards making the most of BERT in neural machine translation. In *Proc. of AAAI*.

Rong Ye, Mingxuan Wang, and Lei Li. 2021. End-to-end speech translation via cross-modal progressive training. In *Proc. of INTERSPEECH*.

Jinhua Zhu, Yingce Xia, Lijun Wu, Di He, Tao Qin, Wengang Zhou, Houqiang Li, and Tie-Yan Liu. 2020. Incorporating BERT into neural machine translation. In *Proc. of ICLR*.

Prosody: Models, Methods and Applications

Nigel G. Ward
University of Texas at El Paso
nigelward@acm.org

Gina-Anne Levow
University of Washington
levow@uw.edu

1 Motivation

Prosody is essential in human interaction, enabling people to show interest, establish rapport, efficiently convey nuances of attitude or intent, and so on.

This tutorial will overview the computational modeling of prosody, including recent advances and diverse actual and potential applications.

We define prosody broadly, as the aspects of spoken utterances that are not governed by segmental contrasts. Some applications that exploit prosodic knowledge have recently shown superhuman performance, and our ability to effectively model prosody is rapidly advancing. Yet prosody remains challenging to work with because it operates close to the limits of conscious introspection, and because most spoken utterances involve multiple prosodic dimensions simultaneously serving multiple communicative functions. Intuitions about prosody are often a weak guide for applied work, but a little bit of basic knowledge can go a long way.

2 Outline

Human Fundamentals: articulatory and perceptual aspects [20 minutes]

Processing Fundamentals: prosodic feature computation and feature sets, including issues of individual variation and normalization [30 minutes]

Phonological and Structural Aspects: tone, stress, boundaries, etc. [40 minutes]

Paralinguistic Functions [20 minutes]

Pragmatic Functions, including turn taking, topic structuring, and stance taking functions [70 minutes]

. . . and interleaved with the above . . .

Representations, Models, and Algorithms, including such recent developments as superpositional modeling, the use of unsupervised methods, and sequence-to-sequence algorithms

Current Trends, including modeling prosody beyond just intonation, representing prosodic knowledge with constructions of multiple prosodic features in specific temporal configurations, and modeling multispeaker phenomenon

Historical Perspectives, briefly, including the long view but focusing on the last 5-10 years

Tools and Resources, and common pitfalls in their uses

Challenges, both short term and long term

Applications, including speech synthesis, speech recognition, diagnosis of medical conditions, inference of speaker sentiments, states and intentions, adaptation in dialog, information retrieval, speaker identification, skills training and assessment

Short Exercises (non-computational)

Throughout, diversity will be a recurring theme, in terms of the different ways in which prosody serves different kinds of functions, in terms of differences in prosodic behaviors across genres, in terms of prosody in typologically-different languages, and in terms of diverse applications.

3 Target Audiences

We envisage three main audiences.

1. Many students of computational linguistics have little exposure to prosody, and what they do

Proceedings of the Joint Conference of the 59th Annual Meeting of the Association for Computational Linguistics and the 11th International Joint Conference on Natural Language Processing: Tutorial Abstracts, pages 26–28, August 1st, 2021.

learn is usually 10 to 20 years out of date. There are great opportunities in industry for speech scientists and engineers (as distinct from language scientists and engineers in general) with unmet needs in the tech giants, in traditional industries, and in start ups. The rise of conversational agents has greatly increased student interest in speech, and we hope that our tutorial will help satisfy their curiosity and open doors for students who might not otherwise even be considered for positions in this field. While today most aspects of speech processing are handled by algorithms which are also used for other computational linguistics purposes, prosody, as a phenomenon entirely unique to the spoken language, has different properties and different functions from the rest of language, and is thus possibly the most important aspect of speech for students to learn about.

2. Developers of language processing applications can easily over- or under-estimate the power of prosody and the ease of using it. In this tutorial we will aim to give participants the ability to, given an application potentially exploiting prosody, evaluate the relevance, feasibility and likely value of various approaches and methods.

3. Research team leaders and Ph.D. students may consider starting a research project that involves prosody, whether centrally or marginally. This tutorial will identify key opportunities, issues, and challenges.

But almost anyone in computational linguistics may benefit from this tutorial, as prosody is a topic of wide cross-cutting relevance, including to grammar, discourse, pragmatics, nonverbal communication, and language learning. Considering the roles and nature of prosody may provide insight and new ways to look at both classic problems and emerging applications, such as those involving multimodalilty, hard realtime performance, and perceptions of systems as human-like agents.

This tutorial will be at an introductory level, assuming no previous knowledge of prosody. We expect that most participants will be familiar with basic issues in modeling language and in standard methods for learning from data, but no specific knowledge will be assumed. Familiarity with basic phonetics and phonology would be helpful, but is again not assumed.

4 Small Reading List

An Introduction to English Phonetics, 2nd Edition, Richard A. Ogden, Edinburgh University Press, 2017. Chapter 4.

Analysing Conversation: An introduction to prosody. Beatrice Szczepek Reed. Palgrave Macmillan, 2010. Chapter 2.

The Geneva Minimalistic Acoustic Parameter Set. Florian Eyben, Klaus Scherrer et al. *IEEE Transactions on Affective Computing* 7:2, pp 193-194, 2016. sections 3.1 and 3.2.

Prosody in Context: A review. Jennifer Cole. *Language, Cognition and Neuroscience*, 30:1-2, 1-31, 2015.

Speech Prosody: theories, models and analysis. Yi Xu. In *Courses on Speech Prosody*, A. R. Meireles (ed), Cambridge Scholars Press, 2015 pp 146-177.

Prosodic Patterns in English Conversation. Nigel G. Ward. Cambridge University Press, 2019. Chapter 8.

Speech and Language Processing, 3nd Edition draft. Dan Jurafsky and James H. Martin, 2021. Section 26.2

5 Presenters

Nigel Ward
Computer Science
University of Texas at El Paso
nigelward@acm.org
http://www.cs.utep.edu/nigel/

Gina-Anne Levow
Linguistics
University of Washington
levow@uw.edu
http://faculty.washington.edu/levow

Ward's research interests lie at the intersection of spoken dialog and prosody. His expertise includes applications of prosody in information retrieval, speech recognition, dialog systems, and language learning. He is known for the creation of a robust prosodic feature set for processing prosody in dialog data, for the computational modeling of prosodic constructions, and for data-backed descriptions of the prosody of dialog in English, Mandarin, Spanish and Japanese. He is the author of *Prosodic Patterns in English Conversation* (Cambridge University Press, 2019) and is for 2018-2022 Chair of the Speech Prosody Special

Interest Group of the International Speech Communication Association.

Levow's research concentrates on the use of intonation in spoken dialog, and her interests range over natural language processing, spoken language systems, and human-computer interfaces. Her expertise includes examination of the prosodic correlates of stance taking, modeling dysarthria, describing and modeling endangered languages, identifying the prosodic markers of turn taking in Arabic, Spanish and English, and developing minimally supervised machine learning techniques to recognize lexical tones in Mandarin, Cantonese, isiZulu, and isiXhosa.

6 Resources

Available at http://www.cs.utep.edu/nigel/intro-to-prosody/ .

Recognizing Multimodal Entailment

Cesar Ilharco[γ] **Afsaneh Shirazi**[γ] **Arjun Gopalan**[ρ] **Arsha Nagrani**[ρ] **Blaž Bratanič**[γ]
Chris Bregler[ρ] **Christina Liu**[ρ] **Felipe Ferreira**[γ] **Gabriek Barcik**[ρ] **Gabriel Ilharco**[ω]
Georg Osang[α] **Jannis Bulian**[ρ] **Jared Frank**[γ] **Lucas Smaira**[δ] **Qin Cao**[ρ]
Ricardo Marino[γ] **Roma Patel**[β] **Thomas Leung**[ρ] **Vaiva Imbrasaite**[ρ]

[γ]Google [ρ]Google Research [β]Brown University [ω]University of Washington [α]IST Austria [δ]DeepMind

[γρδ]{ ilharco, afsaneh, arjung, anagrani, blazb, bregler, christinafunk, felipeg, gbarcik, jbulian, jaredfrank, lsmaira, qincao, ricm, leungt, vimbrasaite } @google.com
[ω]gamaga@cs.washington.edu, [α]georg.osang@ist.ac.at, [β]roma_patel1@brown.edu

Abstract

How information is created, shared and consumed has changed rapidly in recent decades, in part thanks to new social platforms and technologies on the web. With ever-larger amounts of unstructured and limited labels, organizing and reconciling information from different sources and modalities is a central challenge in machine learning.

This cutting-edge tutorial aims to introduce the multimodal entailment task, which can be useful for detecting semantic alignments when a single modality alone does not suffice for a whole content understanding. Starting with a brief overview of natural language processing, computer vision, structured data and neural graph learning, we lay the foundations for the multimodal sections to follow. We then discuss recent multimodal learning literature covering visual, audio and language streams, and explore case studies focusing on tasks which require fine-grained understanding of visual and linguistic semantics question answering, veracity and hatred classification. Finally, we introduce a new dataset for recognizing multimodal entailment, exploring it in a hands-on collaborative section.

Overall, this tutorial gives an overview of multimodal learning, introduces a multimodal entailment dataset, and encourages future research in the topic.

1 Website

multimodal-entailment.github.io

2 Type of the tutorial

Cutting edge.

3 Diversity considerations

- Instructors affiliated in 6 different countries.

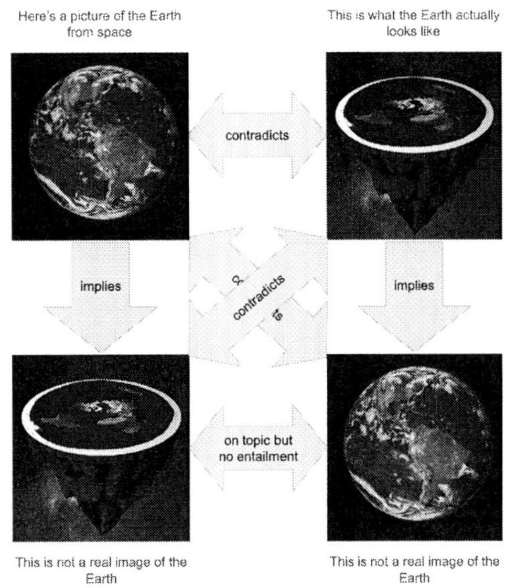

Figure 1: Example of multimodal entailment where texts or images alone would not suffice for semantic understanding or pairwise classifications.

- 3 academia and 3 industry affiliations.
- 6 female organizers.
- 5 female instructors.
- Participation of senior (up to Research Director) and junior (PhD candidate) instructors.
- Recognizing Multimodal Entailment can help with automated fact-checking, prompting for (re)focusing on traditionally underserved audiences (Scheufele and Krause, 2019).

4 Prerequisites

- Programming or other tools: Familiarity with Python and a high level machine learning framework.
- Machine Learning: Basic understanding of deep learning for Natural Language Processing and Computer Vision is desired, but not

Proceedings of the Joint Conference of the 59th Annual Meeting of the Association for Computational Linguistics and the 11th International Joint Conference on Natural Language Processing: Tutorial Abstracts, pages 29–30, August 1st, 2021.

critical for a successful completion of the tutorial.

5 Reading list

Bui et al. (2017); Vaswani et al. (2017); Peters et al. (2018); Devlin et al. (2018); Lan et al. (2019); Raffel et al. (2019); Ngiam et al. (2011); Lu et al. (2019a,b); Tan and Bansal (2019); Su et al. (2019); Sun et al. (2019b,a); Alayrac et al. (2020).

6 Tutorial presenters

Afsaneh Shirazi, Arjun Gopalan, Arsha Nagrani, Cesar Ilharco, Christina Liu, Gabriel Barcik, Jannis Bulian, Jared Frank, Lucas Smaira, Qin Cao, Ricardo Marino and Roma Patel.

7 Open access

We agree to allow the publication of slides and video recording of the tutorial in the ACL Anthology. Teaching materials will be openly available.

8 Acknowledgements

We would like to thank Abby Schantz, Abe Ittycheriah, Aliaksei Severyn, Allan Heydon, Aly Grealish, Andrey Vlasov, Arkaitz Zubiaga, Ashwin Kakarla, Chen Sun, Clayton Williams, Cong Yu, Cordelia Schmid, Da-Cheng Juan, Dan Finnie, Dani Valevski, Daniel Rocha, David Price, David Sklar, Devi Krishna, Elena Kochkina, Enrique Alfonseca, Françoise Beaufays, Isabelle Augenstein, Jialu Liu, John Cantwell, John Palowitch, Jordan Boyd-Graber, Lei Shi, Luís Valente, Maria Voitovich, Mehmet Aktuna, Mogan Brown, Mor Naaman, Natalia P, Nidhi Hebbar, Pete Aykroyd, Rahul Sukthankar, Richa Dixit, Steve Pucci, Tania Bedrax-Weiss, Tobias Kaufmann, Tom Boulos, Tu Tsao, Vladimir Chtchetkine, Yair Kurzion, Yifan Xu and Zach Hynes.

References

Jean-Baptiste Alayrac, Adrià Recasens, Rosalia Schneider, Relja Arandjelović, Jason Ramapuram, Jeffrey De Fauw, Lucas Smaira, Sander Dieleman, and Andrew Zisserman. 2020. Self-supervised multimodal versatile networks.

Thang D. Bui, Sujith Ravi, and Vivek Ramavajjala. 2017. Neural graph machines: Learning neural networks using graphs.

Jacob Devlin, Ming-Wei Chang, Kenton Lee, and Kristina Toutanova. 2018. Bert: Pre-training of deep bidirectional transformers for language understanding. *arXiv preprint arXiv:1810.04805*.

Zhenzhong Lan, Mingda Chen, Sebastian Goodman, Kevin Gimpel, Piyush Sharma, and Radu Soricut. 2019. Albert: A lite bert for self-supervised learning of language representations.

Jiasen Lu, Dhruv Batra, Devi Parikh, and Stefan Lee. 2019a. Vilbert: Pretraining task-agnostic visiolinguistic representations for vision-and-language tasks.

Jiasen Lu, Vedanuj Goswami, Marcus Rohrbach, Devi Parikh, and Stefan Lee. 2019b. 12-in-1: Multi-task vision and language representation learning.

Jiquan Ngiam, Aditya Khosla, Mingyu Kim, Juhan Nam, Honglak Lee, and Andrew Y Ng. 2011. Multimodal deep learning. In *Proceedings of the 28th international conference on machine learning (ICML-11)*, pages 689–696.

Matthew E Peters, Mark Neumann, Mohit Iyyer, Matt Gardner, Christopher Clark, Kenton Lee, and Luke Zettlemoyer. 2018. Deep contextualized word representations. *arXiv preprint arXiv:1802.05365*.

Colin Raffel, Noam Shazeer, Adam Roberts, Katherine Lee, Sharan Narang, Michael Matena, Yanqi Zhou, Wei Li, and Peter J. Liu. 2019. Exploring the limits of transfer learning with a unified text-to-text transformer.

Dietram A. Scheufele and Nicole M. Krause. 2019. Science audiences, misinformation, and fake news. *Proceedings of the National Academy of Sciences*, 116(16):7662–7669.

Weijie Su, Xizhou Zhu, Yue Cao, Bin Li, Lewei Lu, Furu Wei, and Jifeng Dai. 2019. Vl-bert: Pre-training of generic visual-linguistic representations.

Chen Sun, Fabien Baradel, Kevin Murphy, and Cordelia Schmid. 2019a. Learning video representations using contrastive bidirectional transformer.

Chen Sun, Austin Myers, Carl Vondrick, Kevin Murphy, and Cordelia Schmid. 2019b. Videobert: A joint model for video and language representation learning.

Hao Tan and Mohit Bansal. 2019. Lxmert: Learning cross-modality encoder representations from transformers. *Proceedings of the 2019 Conference on Empirical Methods in Natural Language Processing and the 9th International Joint Conference on Natural Language Processing (EMNLP-IJCNLP)*.

Ashish Vaswani, Noam Shazeer, Niki Parmar, Jakob Uszkoreit, Llion Jones, Aidan N Gomez, Łukasz Kaiser, and Illia Polosukhin. 2017. Attention is all you need. In *Advances in neural information processing systems*, pages 5998–6008.

Author Index

Association for Computational Linguistics
209 N. Eighth Street
Stroudsburg, Pennsylvania 18360

ISBN 978-1-7138-3312-3

CURRAN ASSOCIATES INC.
proceedings.com